Progressive Web Apps

Progressive Web Apps

DEAN ALAN HUME

FOREWORD BY ADDY OSMANI

MANNING

SHELTER ISLAND

For online information and ordering of this and other Manning books, please visit www.manning.com. The publisher offers discounts on this book when ordered in quantity. For more information, please contact

> Special Sales Department
> Manning Publications Co.
> 20 Baldwin Road
> PO Box 761
> Shelter Island, NY 11964
> Email: orders@manning.com

Manning Publications Co.	Development editor: Jennifer Stout
20 Baldwin Road	Technical development editor: Marius Butuc
PO Box 761	Project editor: Janet Vail
Shelter Island, NY 11964	Copyeditor: Corbin Collins
	Proofreader: Melody Dolab
	Technical proofreader: Alexey Galiullin
	Typesetter: Dennis Dalinnik
	Cover designer: Marija Tudor

ISBN: 9781617294587
Printed in the United States of America
1 2 3 4 5 6 7 8 9 10 – EBM – 22 21 20 19 18 17

In memory of Frank Hume—"Keep 'em flying"

brief contents

contents

foreword

For many global brands, including Twitter and Forbes, a Progressive Web App (PWA) is now the default way to ship a modern mobile web experience. PWAs can provide fast, compelling journeys similar to what can be achieved with a native app—but they're also discoverable and accessible to everyone via the mobile web.

Users re-engage with PWAs using features like push notifications and Add to Homescreen, which have enabled PWAs like Lancôme to see a 16% increase in year-on-year revenue since launching in October 2016. PWAs also support instant and offline loading experiences on repeat visits, enabling productivity on-the-go, even with spotty network connectivity.

Dean Hume's excellent *Progressive Web Apps* takes a practical, example-driven approach to learning how PWAs can help you build fast, engaging sites. You'll find each PWA feature presented in a tidy, independent section that highlights why the feature can provide user value, how to use it, and best practices learned from PWAs that have shipped to production.

As an early adopter of PWAs, Dean is aware of some of the most valuable tips and tricks for shipping a mobile site that efficiently uses these new features. I'm happy to recommend *Progressive Web Apps* and hope it helps you unlock the potential for fantastic user experiences on mobile.

—ADDY OSMANI, engineering manager working on PWAs at Google

preface

I've been fortunate to have been a web developer for almost 15 years now. The web has changed a lot since I first started out, and with each year that passes, it feels like it's getting better and better.

About five years ago, I was sitting in a conference room listening to Google's Alex Russell talk about Service Workers and how they were the next big thing that was going to change the web. Many people in the audience (me included) weren't too sure about this newfangled feature and the benefits it might bring to the web. But true to his word, Service Workers and now Progressive Web Apps (PWAs) are here to stay and have forever changed the web for good.

I remember when I first started experimenting with PWAs. At first, things seemed a little complicated, but as soon as I wrote my first working Service Worker it all seemed to click. That "a-ha!" moment struck, and I realized how powerful these features could really be. Ever since then, I've been hooked.

I'm wholly passionate about web performance and producing fast web pages that delight users. In fact, many years ago, I wrote a book with Manning about web performance and ASP.NET websites (who knew, right?) For me personally, the best thing about PWAs is that they help you build fast, resilient, and engaging web applications that delight your users. By the time you're finished reading this book, I hope that you too have that "a-ha!" moment and that you're as passionate about PWAs as I am.

acknowledgments

I want to start by thanking my wonderful wife Emily for all of the encouragement while I was writing this book. I love bouncing ideas off of you and value your opinion. I regularly come running to you with crazy, hairbrained ideas, and you're always patient enough to listen to them!

Writing this book was a truly enjoyable experience, and I would like to say a very special thanks to the awesome Jennifer Stout for all your help. Your cool calmness during the editing process made it a breeze—plus it's been fun, too! We're like the Han Solo and Chewbacca of the writing world (I'm Chewie). This is the third book we've worked on together, and I hope there will be more to come.

Many of the technical aspects of this book wouldn't have been possible without the help of Marius Butuc. Thank you, Marius, for your useful insights, technical guidance, and all-around great advice, and it's been great to see you as excited about this book as I am.

As always, a special thanks to my buddy Robin Osborne. Early morning breakfast and inspiration wouldn't be the same without you—thanks for the encouragement. Two Huevos al Benny's, please!

I'm also extremely grateful to all the technical reviewers who helped shape and improve this book. Addy Osmani, Jake Archibald, and Patrick Haman—thank you for all your help. You provided feedback, gave ideas, and are just plain awesome. Thanks, too, to technical proofreader Alexey Galiullin and all the book's reviewers, including Al Pezewski, Birnou Sébarte, David Krief, Devang Paliwal, Evan Wallace, Goran Ore,

xvii

Kamal Raj, Keith Donaldson, Ken W. Alger, Kim Lokøy, Laura Steadman, Michal Paszkiewicz, and Ron Chloupek.

Finally, thank you for purchasing this book! I hope that you enjoy reading it as much as I enjoyed writing it.

about this book

Progressive Web Apps was written to help you use the amazing features of Progressive Web Apps (PWAs) to build fast, engaging, and resilient web applications. The book begins by focusing on the basics of PWAs and soon dives into their core features, demonstrating how to implement them on your own websites. In the various chapters, the book dissects existing PWAs that some large organizations around the world have built and explores different tips and tricks that you can use to improve your own PWAs.

Progressive Web Apps is for web developers who are looking to take their web development to the next level. Both beginners and experienced web developers will learn what PWAs are all about and how to use their features to enhance their websites. Although plenty of blog posts and docs about this topic exist online, this book brings together everything in a clear, easy-to-follow format that will benefit anyone wanting to learn more about PWAs. A prior knowledge of web development will help you while reading through the various chapters in this book, but overall you don't need to be an expert. As you work through this book, you'll take a basic web application and slowly add new PWA features to it.

How this book is organized

This book has 11 chapters divided into five parts.

Part 1 starts with the basics and explains everything you need to know about the foundations of PWAs:

- Chapter 1 discusses PWAs and builds a business case for why they're so important to the modern web developer. The chapter also dives into Service Workers, which play a key role in the creation of PWAs.
- Chapter 2 takes the first steps toward building PWAs and discusses different architectural approaches you can use when building them. Here we also dissect an existing PWA step-by-step and see how organizations around the world are starting to benefit from their features.

Part 2 covers using the power of Service Workers to build faster web applications:

- Chapter 3 looks at the basics of Service Worker caching and then gets into some of the more advanced use cases of caching on the web.
- Chapter 4 explores the Fetch API and explains how you can tap into it to speed up the load times of your PWAs. It also looks at two clever techniques using WebP images and the Save-Data header to reduce the overall weight of web pages.

Part 3 covers the features that will help you create engaging PWAs:

- Chapter 5 describes how you can use the web app manifest file to build an engaging PWA. We'll look into a feature known as Add to Homescreen and consider some more advanced techniques for getting the most out of this great feature.
- Chapter 6 explains what push notifications are and how to use them to truly engage with your users. It goes through a step-by-step example that demonstrates how you can begin implementing your own push notifications.

Part 4 covers techniques that can be used to build resilient PWAs:

- Chapter 7 covers offline browsing and explains how to unlock the cache within the browser to start building truly offline applications.
- Chapter 8 talks about building PWAs that cater to situations where the user has a troublesome network connection. You'll learn the best techniques for building resilient web apps that work with poor or unreliable network connections.
- Chapter 9 describes the techniques used to build offline web applications that are able to synchronize data when they re-establish network connectivity. This chapter looks at an API known as BackgroundSync and demonstrates how to build PWAs that use this powerful feature.

Part 5 covers the future of PWAs and the many great, new features that are currently available for developers to start using today:

- Chapter 10 discusses the Web Stream API and explains why it's so powerful. The chapter also demonstrates how to use this API to supercharge your page load times.

- Chapter 11 covers some of the most common questions I'm asked and attempts to answer them as clearly and thoroughly as possible.
- The final chapter, chapter 12, explores the future of PWAs and a few of the new APIs that are either in development or are currently available to experiment with.

In general, developers who are entirely new to PWAs should read the first two chapters for a basic understanding of their inner workings and how to correctly set up the environment for development. From the start of the book, you create a sample application and build on it in each chapter. That said, this book was written so that you can flip between chapters and read out of order, picking and choosing depending on the topics that interest you. But for a well-rounded understanding of the many great features of PWAs, I recommend reading all the chapters.

Code conventions and downloads

The code for all numbered listings is available for download from www.manning.com/ books/progressive-web-apps and is also on GitHub at https://github.com/dean-hume/progressive-web-apps-book.

About the author

 DEAN ALAN HUME is an author, blogger, software developer, and Google developer expert. He has written numerous articles and given dozens of presentations, and is the author of *Fast ASP.NET Websites* (Manning, 2013) and *Building Great Startup Teams* (Blurb, 2017). He also contributed to the book *A Career On The Web: On the Road to Success* (Smashing Magazine, 2015). A software developer at heart, Dean is passionate about web performance and regularly writes articles based on all things software development on his blog deanhume.com. He collects hobbies, including surfing, snowboarding, boxing, and participating in triathlons; currently, he's learning to brew beer.

Book forum

Purchase of *Progressive Web Apps* includes free access to a private web forum run by Manning Publications where you can make comments about the book, ask technical questions, and receive help from the author and from other users. To access the forum, go to https://forums.manning.com/forums/progressive-web-apps. You can also learn more about Manning's forums and the rules of conduct at https://forums.manning.com/forums/about.

Manning's commitment to our readers is to provide a venue where a meaningful dialogue between individual readers and between readers and the author can take place. It is not a commitment to any specific amount of participation on the part of the author, whose contribution to the forum remains voluntary (and unpaid). We suggest you try asking the author some challenging questions lest his interest stray! The forum and the archives of previous discussions will be accessible from the publisher's website as long as the book is in print.

About the cover

The figure on the cover of Progressive Web Apps is captioned "Habit of an Ethiopian, in 1581." The illustration is taken from Thomas Jefferys' *A Collection of the Dresses of Different Nations, Ancient and Modern* (four volumes), London, published between 1757 and 1772. The title page states that these are hand-colored copperplate engravings, heightened with gum arabic. Thomas Jefferys (1719–1771) was called "Geographer to King George III." He was an English cartographer who was the leading map supplier of his day. He engraved and printed maps for government and other official bodies and produced a wide range of commercial maps and atlases, especially of North America. His work as a mapmaker sparked an interest in local dress customs of the lands he surveyed and mapped, which are brilliantly displayed in this collection.

Fascination with faraway lands and travel for pleasure were relatively new phenomena in the late 18th century and collections such as this one were popular, introducing both the tourist as well as the armchair traveler to the inhabitants of other countries. The diversity of the drawings in Jefferys' volumes speaks vividly of the uniqueness and individuality of the world's nations some 200 years ago. Dress codes have changed since then and the diversity by region and country, so rich at the time, has faded away. It is now often hard to tell the inhabitant of one continent from another. Perhaps, trying to view it optimistically, we have traded a cultural and visual diversity for a more varied personal life, or a more varied and interesting intellectual and technical life.

At a time when it is hard to tell one computer book from another, Manning celebrates the inventiveness and initiative of the computer business with book covers based on the rich diversity of regional life of two centuries ago, brought back to life by Jeffreys' pictures.

Part 1

Defining Progressive Web Apps

In 2015, the International Telecommunication Union estimated that about 3.2 billion people, or almost half of the world's population, would be online by the end of that year. Think about that number for a second. 3.2 billion people. That's about 32,000 football stadiums full of people! It almost seems too big to comprehend. As these people come online they will be doing so on different devices with different connection speeds and ever-changing conditions. As web developers, trying to cater to all these different scenarios seems daunting to say the least. This is where Progressive Web Apps (PWAs) come in. They provide us as developers with the ability to build faster, more resilient, and more engaging websites that can be accessed by billions around the world. The chapters in this first part of the book dive straight into defining exactly what PWAs are and what they can do.

In chapter 1, you'll learn about the benefits of PWAs. We'll look at businesses that are already harnessing the power of PWAs to improve their users' browsing experience. We'll also dissect a real-world PWA and look at how companies such as Twitter and Flipkart have built their own PWAs. A key component of PWAs is the Service Worker, and I'll be covering this topic in depth, as well as the lifecycle that Service Workers go through when loaded in a web browser.

Chapter 2 begins by looking at the different architectural approaches you can use when building a PWA and how to best structure your code. We'll look at two different approaches: "picking and choosing vitamins" or the Application

Shell Architecture, both of which can be adapted to suit the needs of your project. The best thing about PWAs is that you don't have to rewrite your existing web applications to start using their features—you can add new features whenever you feel that they'll benefit the user and provide them with an enhanced experience. The chapter finishes by dissecting an existing PWA, known as Twitter Lite, which was developed by the team at Twitter.

By the end of part 1, you should have a clear understanding of what PWAs are and the benefits they can bring to your users. This first part of the book sets the building blocks for the next part, where we get into coding and building a PWA from scratch.

Understanding Progressive Web Apps

1

Imagine that you had the ability to build a website that worked completely offline, offered your users near instant load times, and yet was secure and resilient to unreliable networks at the same time. Sounds both impossible and amazing! Believe it or not, most modern browsers already have these features built into them—they only need to be unlocked. When you build a website that takes advantage of these powerful features, you have what is known as a Progressive Web App (PWA).

In this chapter, you'll learn what makes a web app *progressive* and how you can unlock the powerful functionality that already lies within your browser. By the end of the chapter, you'll have a clear understanding of the benefits that PWAs bring to users and why they are such a game-changer for the web. Finally, we'll look at a real-life example of a company that's already benefitting from using a PWA.

1.1   *What's the big deal with Progressive Web Apps?*

Way back during Christmas 1990, Sir Tim Berners-Lee and his team at CERN built all the tools necessary for a working web. They created HTTP, HTML, and the world's first web browser, called WorldWideWeb.[1] The web pages that the first browser could run were simple plain-text pages with hyperlinks. In fact, those first web pages are still online and available to view today.

Fast-forward a few decades, and our browsers aren't that different. Sure, we have features such as CSS and JavaScript, but we still build with HTML, HTTP, and the other blocks that Berners-Lee and his team created all those years ago. These brilliant building blocks mean that the web has been able to grow at a remarkable rate. But

---

[1] https://en.wikipedia.org/wiki/History_of_the_World_Wide_Web

the number of devices we use to access web pages has also grown remarkably over the years. Whether on the go or sitting at their desks, your users have unparalleled access to information at their fingertips. Our expectations for the web have never been higher.

Although our mobile devices have become more powerful, our mobile networks haven't always been able to keep up with the demand. If you own a smartphone, you know how flaky a mobile connection can be. 2G, 3G, or 4G are all great, but they often lose connection or leave us with poor network speeds. If your business is reliant on the web, this is a problem you need to solve.

Historically speaking, native apps (installed on your phone) have been able to offer a much better overall user experience—you download the app and it loads instantly. If there's no network connection, it's not the end of the world. You already have most of the resources on your device that you need to serve your customer. This ability to offer a resilient, engaging experience has led to an explosion in the number of native apps. There are currently over 4 million combined native apps in the Apple App Store and the Google Play Store.[2]

Historically speaking, the web hasn't been able to offer these same great features such as offline capabilities, instant load times, and improved reliability. This is where PWAs are a game-changer. Major browser vendors have been working together to improve the way we build for the web and have created a new set of features that give web developers the ability to create fast, reliable, and engaging websites. A PWA should be all of these things:

- Responsive
- Connectivity-independent
- Interactive with a feel like a native app's
- Always up-to-date
- Safe
- Discoverable
- Re-engageable
- Installable
- Linkable

As web developers, this is a shift in mindset from the way we traditionally approach building a website. It means we can start building websites that can cope with changing network conditions or zero connectivity. It also means that we can build websites that are more engaging for our users and offer those users a first-class browsing experience.

At this point, you may be thinking, *this is crazy*! What about older browsers that don't support these features? One of the best things about PWAs is that they're truly progressive. If you build a PWA, it will still work as a normal website even if an older browser doesn't support it. The technologies that drive PWAs have been designed so that it only enhances the experience if the browser is capable of supporting the features.

---

[2] www.statista.com/statistics/276623/number-of-apps-available-in-leading-app-stores/

If your user's device does support them, they get all the extra benefits and more improved features. Either way, it's a win-win situation for you and your users.

1.2 PWA basics

What exactly makes up a Progressive Web App? We've talked about their features and principles, but what makes something a *Progressive* Web App? At their simplest, PWAs are normal websites created with the technologies we know and love as web developers—HTML, CSS, and JavaScript—but they go a few steps further and offer users an enhanced experience. I like the way Alex Russell, a developer on the Google Chrome team, describes them: "These apps aren't packaged and deployed through stores, they're just websites that took all the right vitamins."

PWAs point to a file known as a *manifest* file that contains information about the website, including its icons, background screen, colors, and default orientation. (In chapter 6, you'll learn how to make your website more engaging using manifest files.)

PWAs use an important new feature known as Service Workers to let you tap into network requests and build better web experiences. As you progress through this chapter, you'll learn more about them and the improvements they bring to the browser. A PWA will also let you "save" it to the home screen of your device. It will appear exactly as a native app would, giving you easy access to the web app at the touch of a button (more on this in chapter 6).

A PWA should also be able to work offline. Using Service Workers, you can selectively cache parts of your site to provide an offline experience. If you've browsed most websites today without an internet connection, you've probably seen a screen that looks similar to figure 1.1.

Users no longer need to face the dreaded "No internet connection" screen. Using Service Workers, you can intercept and cache any network requests to and from your site. Whether you're building

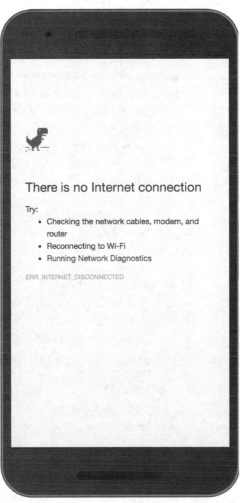

Figure 1.1   The offline screen can be frustrating if you need to access information in a hurry.

websites for mobile, desktop, or tablet devices, you have control over how you want to respond to requests with or without a network connection. (We'll dive into caching in chapter 3 and build an offline web page in chapter 8.)

PWAs are more than a set of great new features—they're a way to build better websites. They're also quickly becoming a set of best practices. The steps you take to build a PWA will benefit anyone who visits your website, regardless of which device they choose to use.

Once you've unlocked the basic building blocks needed to start building PWAs, you'll quickly find that the more advanced examples don't seem that advanced after all. Once you get into the swing of building Progressive Web Apps, you'll how easy it is.

1.2.1   *Building a business case for Progressive Web Apps*

As a developer, I know how exciting it can be when a new technology or set of features comes along. The urge to dive right in and introduce the latest and greatest library or framework into your website can often overshadow the value it brings to a business. Believe it or not, PWAs bring real value to your users and can make a website more engaging, resilient, and even faster.

The best thing about a PWA is that you can start enhancing your existing web application one feature at a time. The collection of technologies we'll discuss throughout this book can be applied to any existing website or even to a new web application you may be building. Regardless of the stack you choose to develop your website, PWAs work hand-in-hand with your solution because they're based on HTML, CSS, and JavaScript.

Now that you have a basic understanding of PWAs, let's stop for a second and imagine the possibilities of what you can build. Let's say your online business is a newspaper that people visit to discover more about their local area. If you know that people regularly visit your site and read multiple pages, why not cache those pages ahead of time for them so they can read the information completely offline? Or imagine your web app is for a charity that has volunteers working in areas with limited or no connectivity. The features of a PWA would allow you to build an offline app that lets them collect information in the field with no network connection. As soon as they come back to the office or to an area with connectivity, the data can sync back to the server. PWAs are a game-changer for web developers, and I'm personally excited about the features they'll bring to the web.

I mentioned that you can save a PWA to the home screen of your device. Once saved, its icon appears on the home screen and allows your website to be accessible at the touch of a button.

In 2015, Flipkart, India's largest e-commerce site, began building Flipkart Lite, a PWA that combines the best of the web and the best of the Flipkart native app. If you head over to flipkart.com in your browser, you'll see exactly why this website is so successful. The user experience is impressive: the site is fast, works offline, and is enjoyable to use. By building its site as a PWA, Flipkart was able to display an Add to

Homescreen banner (see figure 1.2). Users that arrived via the Add to Homescreen icon were 70% more likely to purchase on the site.[3]

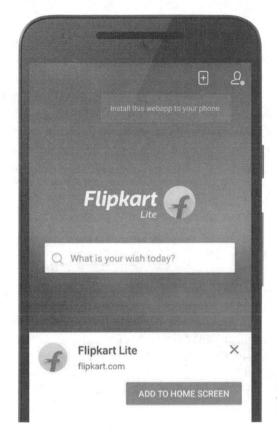

Figure 1.2 The Add to Homescreen functionality can be a great way to re-engage with your users.

Any new native application entering the App Store or Google Play becomes a grain of sand on a beach. As of June 2016, two million apps live in each store at any given time. If you're about to develop a native app aimed at only one of them, you could easily get lost in the many other apps. But because PWAs are websites that took the right vitamins, they're easily discoverable via search engines. People can discover PWAs via social media links or while they browse the web. Building a PWA allows you to reach more people than you could ever achieve with native apps alone, because it's built for any platform capable of running a browser.

I work in a small startup and know how expensive it can be to write an app that works across multiple platforms including iOS, Android, and a website. With PWAs, you only need one team of developers that understands the language of the web. It makes hiring easier and a lot cheaper. That's not to say you shouldn't build a native

---

app, because different users will have different needs, but it does mean that if you wanted to, you could focus on building a great experience for your users on the web and leave it at that.

When it comes to building for the web, a user can easily access a part of your website without having to first download a huge file. A PWA with the right caching techniques in place can save your users data and make functionality available to them in an instant. As more and more users around the world come online, building for the next billion people has never been more important. PWAs help you achieve this by building fast, lean web applications.

If you read software development articles on the web today, you're familiar with the *native versus web* arguments. Which is better? What are the pros and cons of each? Native apps are great in their own right, but the truth is that PWAs aren't only about bringing native features to the web. They solve real problems that businesses are facing and aim to create a truly discoverable, fast, and engaging experience for users.

1.3   Service Workers: The key to PWAs

As mentioned, the key to unlocking the power of PWAs lies in Service Workers. At their core, Service Workers are worker scripts that run in the background. Written in JavaScript with a few lines of code, they enable a developer to intercept network requests, handle push messages, and perform many other tasks.

Best of all, if a user's browser doesn't support Service Workers, it falls back and your website functions as a normal website. PWAs have been described as the "perfect progressive enhancement" because of this. The phrase progressive enhancement refers to the idea that you can build an experience that works anywhere and then enhance the experience for devices that support more advanced features.

1.3.1   Understanding Service Workers

How does a Service Worker...work? Well, in order to make it as simple to understand as possible, I like how Jeff Posnick of Google describes them: "Think of your web requests as planes taking off. Service Worker is the air traffic controller that routes the requests. It can load from the network or even off the cache."

As "air traffic controllers," Service Workers give you total control of each and every web request made from your site, which opens up the possibility for many different use cases. In the same way that an air traffic controller might redirect a plane to another airport, or even delay a landing, a Service Worker enables you to redirect your requests or even stop them completely.

Although Service Workers are written in JavaScript, they're slightly different from your standard JavaScript file. A Service Worker does the following:

- Runs in its own global script context
- Isn't tied to a particular web page
- Isn't able to modify elements in the web page—it has no DOM access
- Is HTTPS only

You don't need to be a JavaScript master to begin experimenting with Service Workers. They're event-driven, and you can pick and choose the events you want to tap into. Once you have a basic understanding of the different events, getting started with Service Workers is easier than you think.

Figure 1.3 illustrates how Service Workers work.

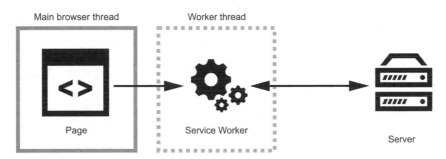

Figure 1.3   Service Workers can intercept incoming and outgoing HTTP requests, giving you total control of your website.

A Service Worker is run in a *worker context*, which means it has no DOM access and runs on a different thread from the main JavaScript that powers your app, so it's not blocking. Service Workers are designed to be fully async, and as a consequence, you can't access things such as synchronous XHR and localStorage. In figure 1.3, you can see that the Service Worker sits on a different thread and is able to intercept network requests. Remember, Service Workers are like air traffic controllers in that they give you total control of network requests coming and going from your website. This ability makes them extremely powerful and allows you to decide how to respond.

1.3.2   *The Service Worker lifecycle*

Before diving in to a coding example, let's look at the different stages a Service Worker goes through in its lifecycle. Imagine a basic website that uses a Service Worker under the hood. The website is a popular blogging platform that millions of writers use every day to share their content.

In its simplest form, the website constantly receives requests for content, including images and videos. To see how the Service Worker lifecycle might fit into this, let's pick one of these millions of interactions to and from the website every single day.

Figure 1.4 shows the Service Worker lifecycle that will take place when a user visits a blogging page on this website.

Let's walk through figure 1.4 step by step to understand how the Service Worker lifecycle fits into this. When a user navigates to a URL for the first time, the server returns a response for the web page. In figure 1.4, you can see that in step 1, the Service Worker begins downloading when you call the `register()` function. During the registration process, the browser will download, parse, and execute the Service Worker

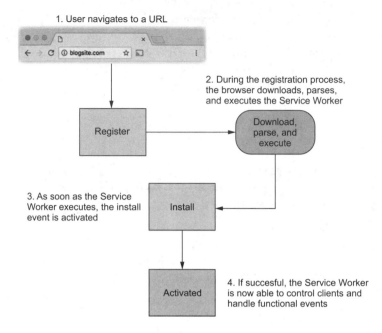

Figure 1.4   The Service Worker lifecycle

(step 2). If at any point during this step there is an error, the `register()` promise will reject, and the Service Worker will be discarded (JavaScript promises will be explained shortly).

As soon as the Service Worker successfully executes, the install event is activated (step 3). One of the great things about Service Workers is that they're *event-based*, which means you can tap into any one of these events. We're going to be using these different events to implement super-fast caching techniques in chapter 3.

Once the install step has completed, the service worker is then *activated* (step 4) and in control of things within its own scope. If all these events in the lifecycle were successful, your service worker is in place and being used.

One way to remember the Service Worker lifecycle is to think of it as a set of traffic lights. During the registration process, the Service Worker is at a red light because it needs to be downloaded and parsed. Next, it is at a yellow light as it's being executed and it's not quite ready to be used yet. If all the steps are successful, your Service Worker is at a green light and ready to be used.

When you load a page for the first time without an active Service Worker, the Service Worker won't handle any requests coming or going. Only after it's been installed and activated is it in control of its own scope. This means the logic inside the Service Worker will only kick in if you refresh the page or navigate to another page.

1.3.3   *A basic Service Worker example*

I'm sure by now you're itching to see what this might look like in code form, so let's get started.

Because a Service Worker is a JavaScript file that runs in a background thread, you reference it in an HTML web page the same way you would any JavaScript file. Imagine you've created a Service Worker file and named it sw.js. To register it, use the code in in the next listing listing in your HTML web page.

Listing 1.1　A basic HTML beb bage

```html
<html>
<head>
<title>The best website ever</title>
</head>
<body>
<script>
// Register the service worker
if ('serviceWorker' in navigator) {
    navigator.serviceWorker.register('/sw.js').then(function(registration) {
    // Registration was successful
    console.log('ServiceWorker registration successful with scope: ',
    registration.scope);
}).catch(function(err) {
    // registration failed :(
    console.log('ServiceWorker registration failed: ', err);
    });
}
</script>
</body>
</html>
```

Check to see if the current browser supports Service Workers.

If it does, register a Service Worker file called sw.js.

Log to the console if successful.

If something goes wrong, catch the error and log to the console.

Inside the script tag, you're first checking to see if Service Workers are supported in the browser. If they are, you register it using the navigator.serviceWorker.register('/sw.js') function, which in turn notifies the browser that it needs to download the Service Worker file. If the registration is successful, it begins the rest of the stages of the Service Worker lifecycle.

In listing 1.1, you may notice that the JavaScript code isn't using callbacks. That's because Service Workers use JavaScript *promises*, which are a clean, readable way to deal with callbacks. A promise represents an operation that hasn't completed yet but is expected to in the future. This lets asynchronous methods return values like synchronous methods and makes writing JavaScript cleaner and also a lot easier to read. Promises can do a great many things, but for now all you need to know is that if something returns a promise, you can attach .then() to the end and include callbacks inside it for success, failure, and so on. Upcoming chapters look at JavaScript promises more closely.

The navigator.serviceWorker.register() function returns a promise, and if the registration is successful you can decide how you want to proceed.

Earlier I mentioned that Service Workers are event-driven, and one of the most powerful features of Service Workers is that they allow you to listen out for any network requests by tapping into different events. One key event is the fetch event. When a fetch event occurs for a resource, you can decide how you want to proceed.

You could alter anything on the outgoing HTTP request or the incoming HTTP response. It's rather simple, but extremely powerful at the same time.

Imagine the following listing inside your Service Worker file.

> **Listing 1.2**

```
self.addEventListener('fetch', function(event) {          ◁——┐ Add an event listener
  if (/\.jpg$/.test(event.request.url)) {                      to the fetch event.
    event.respondWith(fetch('/images/unicorn.jpg'));   ◁——  Check to see if
  }                                                          the HTTP request
});                              Try to fetch an image of a   URL requests a file
                                 unicorn and then respond     ending in .jpg.
                                       with it instead.
```

In listing 1.2, you're listening out for the fetch event, and if the HTTP request is for a JPEG file, you're intercepting it and forcing it to return a picture of a unicorn instead of its original intended URL. The code will do this for each and every HTTP request made for a JPEG file from the website. Although pictures of unicorns are awesome, you probably wouldn't want to do this for a real-world website; your users might not be happy with the result. This example gives you an idea of what Service Workers are capable of. With a few lines of code, you've created a powerful proxy within the browser.

1.3.4   *Security considerations*

In order for a Service Worker to run on a website, it needs to be served over HTTPS. Although that makes it a little tougher to get started using them, there's an important reason for this. Remember the analogy of a Service Worker being like an air traffic controller? With great power comes great responsibility, and in the case of Service Workers, they could be used for malicious purposes, too. If someone were able to register a dodgy Service Worker on your web page, they would be able to hijack connections and redirect them to a malicious endpoint. In fact, the bad guys might be able do whatever they wanted with your HTTP requests. To avoid that, you can only register Service Workers on web pages that are served over HTTPS. This ensures that the web page hasn't been tampered with during its journey through the network.

If you're a web developer who wants to get into building Progressive Web Apps on the side, you may be a little disheartened at this point in the book. Don't be! Getting SSL certificates for your website may have traditionally cost you quite a bit of money, but believe it or not, many free solutions are available to you as a web developer today.

First, if you'd like to test Service Workers on your own computer, you can do so by serving pages from your localhost. They've been built with this feature in mind, which makes it easier for developers to develop locally before deploying their applications live.

If you're ready to release your PWA to the world, there are a few free services that you can use. Let's Encrypt (https://letsencrypt.org) is a new Certificate Authority that's free, automated, and open. You can quickly get started serving your site over HTTPS using Let's Encrypt. To learn more about Let's Encrypt, head over to the Getting Started page at https://letsencrypt.org/getting-started/.

If you use GitHub for source control, as I do, you may have come across GitHub Pages, as shown in figure 1.5. You can host directly from your GitHub repository for basic websites without a back end.

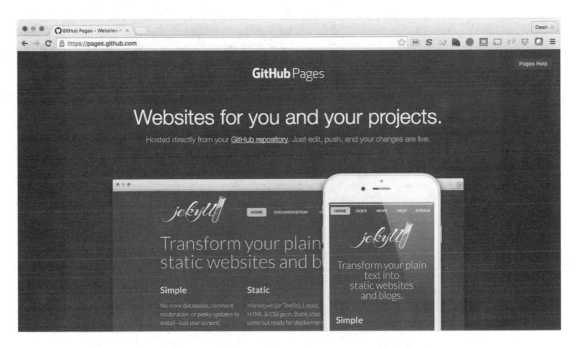

Figure 1.5   GitHub Pages allows you to host a website over SSL directly from a GitHub repository.

The advantage of using GitHub Pages is that by default, your web pages are served over HTTPS. When I first started experimenting with Service Workers, GitHub Pages allowed me to quickly spin up a website and test out an idea in no time.

1.4   *Performance insight: Flipkart*

Earlier in this chapter we looked at an example of an e-commerce company called Flipkart that decided to approach building its website as a PWA. Flipkart is India's largest e-commerce site, and a fast, engaging website is vital to its business success. In emerging markets such as India, the cost of a mobile data package can be quite high, and the mobile networks can be unreliable. For these reasons, many e-commerce companies based in emerging markets need to build light, lean web pages that cater for users on any network.

In 2015, Flipkart adopted an app-only strategy and decided to temporarily shut down its mobile website. The company found it harder and harder to provide a user experience that was as fast and engaging as that of its mobile app. Flipkart decided to rethink its development approach. Its developers were drawn back to the mobile web by the introduction of features that made the mobile web run instantly, work offline, and re-engage users—all the features of a Progressive Web App.

Once they implemented their new PWA, they noticed immediate results. Not only did the site load nearly instantly, but their users were able to continue browsing category pages, reviewing previous searches, and viewing product pages while they were offline. A key metric for Flipkart is data usage, and best of all, when comparing Flipkart Lite to the native app, they found that Flipkart Lite used one-third of the data.

Building a PWA gave them even more benefits. Because the site was fast and engaging, it resulted in users staying three times longer on the site and resulted in a 40% higher engagement rate.[4] Those are some pretty impressive improvements. To see the results for yourself, head over to flipkart.com.

1.5   Summary

In terms of user experience, native applications have been able to offer a much better experience compared to traditional websites.

The web is evolving and there's no reason why we can't offer our users fast, resilient, and engaging web apps. A PWA is capable of providing your users with exactly that.

Service Workers are the key to unlocking the power within your browser. Think of them as air traffic controllers that are capable of intercepting HTTP requests.

The web has always been awesome, but there's no reason why we can't improve it and pass on even greater features to our users. At the end of day, we're building for our users.

---

[4]   https://developers.google.com/web/showcase/2016/pdfs/flipkart.pdf

First steps to building a
Progressive Web App

In chapter 1, you learned that Progressive Web Apps (PWAs) offer a whole new set of features that allow you to build fast, resilient, and engaging web applications. In this chapter, we'll look at some of the best practices for architecting your front-end code when building a PWA. We'll dissect a real-world PWA and look at an overview of its features to gain insight into how you can build your own PWA.

2.1 Build on what you already have

The quote by Alex Russell in chapter 1 (about websites taking their vitamins) sums up the features of a PWA perfectly and ties in nicely with how I felt when I first started to experiment with Service Workers. As soon as I grasped the basic concept of how they worked, there was a light-bulb moment in my head when I realized how powerful they could be. As I started learning more and more about them, I started experimenting with each new PWA feature, or "vitamin," at a time. Learning any new technology can often seem like climbing a mountain. But if you approach your learning about PWAs with the mindset of learning one new feature at a time, you'll have the art of the PWA mastered in no time.

You've undoubtedly put a lot of time and effort into your current projects. Fortunately, building a PWA doesn't mean you have to start all over again from scratch. When I try to improve an existing application, I add a new "vitamin" wherever I feel it will benefit the user and enhance their experience. I like to think of each new PWA feature as Super Mario leveling up every time he eats a new mushroom.

If you have an existing web application that you think would benefit from the features of a PWA, I recommend having a look at a handy tool called Lighthouse (https://github.com/GoogleChrome/lighthouse). It provides useful performance and audit information about your web application, as shown in figure 2.1.

Figure 2.1   The Lighthouse tool is great for auditing and producing performance metrics of a Progressive Web App.

You can use it as a command-line interface or, if your browser of choice is Google Chrome, use the handy Chrome extension. If you run it while pointing to a website, it produces something similar to figure 2.1. The tool runs an audit against your site and produces a helpful checklist of features and performance metrics that you can use to improve your website. If you'd like to use this handy tool and run it against one of your existing sites, head over to github.com/GoogleChrome/lighthouse to find out more.

With the feedback from the Lighthouse tool, you can add new features one at a time and slowly improve the overall experience of your website.

At this point you may be wondering which feature you might want to add to your existing site. Service Workers open up a whole world of possibilities, and deciding where to start can be tricky. As we progress through the rest of this book, each chapter will focus on a new Progressive Web App and will be written in a way that enables you to start building with it regardless of whether you're building for an existing website or a brand new one.

2.2 Front-end architectural approaches to building PWAs

Among developers, there is an ongoing debate over whether it's preferable to build a native app or a web app. Personally, I think that you should choose based on the needs of your users. It shouldn't be a case of PWA versus native apps, but rather, as developers we should always be looking to improve the user experience. As you can imagine, I have a natural bias toward building for the web, but regardless of your preference, if you think of a PWA as a set of best practices, you'll build better websites. For example, if you like developing with React or Angular, you can continue to do so—building a PWA will only enhance the web application and make it faster, more engaging, and more resilient.

Native app developers have long been able to offer their users features that web developers could only dream of, such as the ability to operate offline and respond regardless of network connection. But thanks to the new features that PWAs bring to the web, we can strive to build even better websites. Many native apps are well architected, and as web developers we can learn from their architectural approaches. The next section looks at different architectural approaches you can use in your front-end code when it comes to building PWAs.

2.2.1 The Application Shell Architecture

Lots of great native apps are available today. The Facebook app, for example, provides a nice experience for the user. It lets you know when you're offline, caches your time-line for faster access, and loads in an instant. If you haven't used the Facebook native app in a while, you'll still see an empty UI shell with the header and navigation bar instantly before any of the dynamic content has loaded.

Using the power of Service Workers, there's no reason you can't provide this same experience on the web. With intelligent Service Worker caching, you can cache the UI shell of your website for repeat visits. The new features let you start thinking about and building your websites differently. Whether you're rewriting an existing application or starting from scratch, this approach is something to consider.

You may wonder what I mean by *UI shell*. I mean the minimal HTML, CSS, and JavaScript required to power the user interface. This may be something like the header, footer, and navigation of a site without any dynamic content. If you can load the UI shell and cache it, you can load the dynamic content into the page later. A great example of this in action is Google's Inbox, shown in figure 2.2.

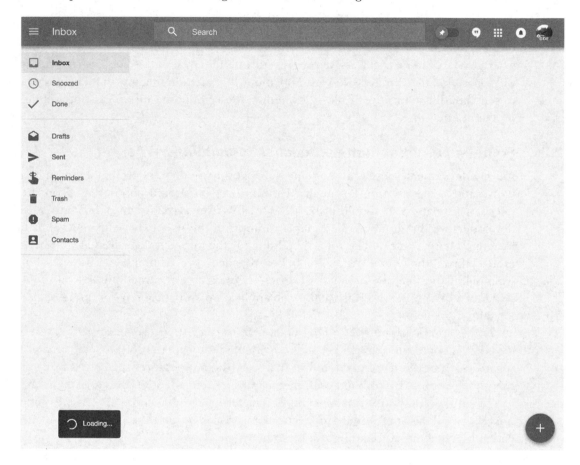

Figure 2.2   Google's Inbox takes advantage of Service Workers to cache the UI shell.

You may already be familiar with Google's Inbox, a handy web application that allows you to organize and send emails. Under the hood it uses Service Workers to cache and provide a super-fast experience for the user. As you can see in figure 2.2, when you first visit the site at you're instantly presented with the UI shell of the website. This is great because the user gets instant feedback and the site feels fast even if you're still waiting for the dynamic content to load. The app gives the perception of speed even if it still takes as long to retrieve content. The user is also notified with a "loading" indicator that something is happening and the site is busy—that's a lot better than waiting for an empty white page to load. Once the shell has loaded, the dynamic contents of the site are fetched and loaded using JavaScript, as shown in figure 2.3.

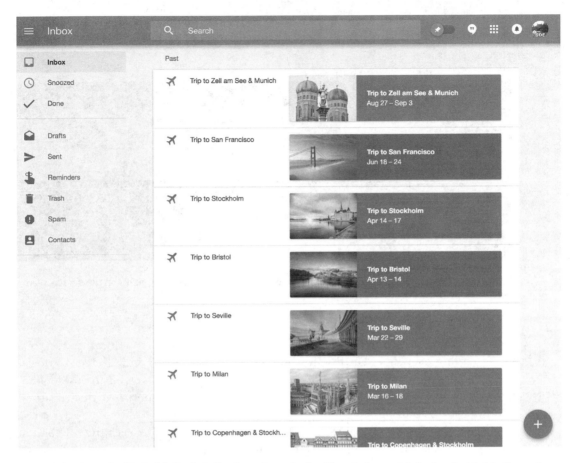

Figure 2.3 Once the UI shell is loaded, the dynamic contents of a website are fetched and added to the page.

Figure 2.3 shows the Google Inbox site once the dynamic content has been loaded and populated in the web app. Using this same technique, you can provide instant loading for repeat visits to your website. You could also cache your application's UI shell so it works offline, allowing you to get meaningful pixels on the screen even if the user doesn't currently have a connection.

In chapter 3, you'll learn how to take advantage of Service Workers to cache your content and provide an offline experience for your users. Throughout this book, you'll build a PWA that will use the Application Shell Architecture. You'll get the chance to download and follow along with the code and build your own app using this approach.

2.2.2 Performance benefits

It's easy to say that a web application loads "instantly" using App Shell Architecture, but what does that mean for a user? How fast is that? To see how quickly a PWA using the App Shell Architecture loads, I used a tool called webpagetest.org to produce the filmstrip in figure 2.4, which shows the load time before and after caching using Service Workers.

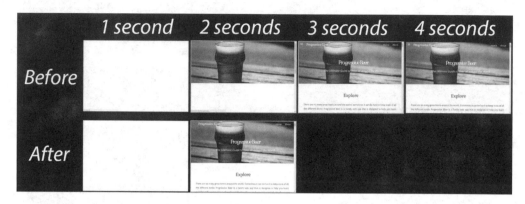

Figure 2.4   The App Shell architecture can provide the user with meaningful pixels on the screen even before the dynamic content has finished loading.

I ran the tool against a PWA I built called Progressive Beer to show a filmstrip view of a PWA loading over time. For the first-time user, the site takes a little longer to download because they're retrieving the assets for the first time. Once all the assets have been downloaded, the first-time user will be able to fully interact with the site at around four seconds.

The repeat user who has an active Service Worker installed sees the UI shell at around 0.5 seconds (500 milliseconds), which is loaded even though the dynamic content hasn't been returned from the server yet. Then the remainder of the dynamic content is loaded and populated onto the screen. The best thing about this approach is that even if there's no connection, a user can still see the UI shell of the site in about half a second—at which point you could present them with something meaningful, such as notifying them that they're offline or providing them with cached content.

Every time they revisit the site, they'll have this enhanced experience that's fast, reliable, and engaging. If you're approaching the development of a new web app, using the Application Shell Architecture can be an efficient way to take advantage of Service Workers.

2.2.3   *The Application Shell Architecture in action*

In chapter 1, we ran through the various stages of the Service Worker lifecycle. It may not have made much sense at the time, but as we look a little deeper into how the Application Shell Architecture works, it will. Remember that using a Service Worker, you can tap into the different events in the Service Worker lifecycle. Figure 2.5 illustrates how to tap into these events.

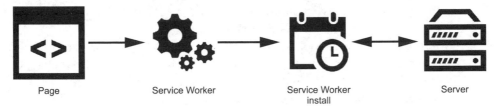

Figure 2.5 During the Service Worker installation step, you can fetch resources and prime the cache for the next visit.

When the user visits the website for the first time, the Service Worker begins downloading and installing itself. During the installation stage, you can tap into this event and prime the cache with all the assets required for the UI shell—the basic HTML page and any CSS or JavaScript that may be required.

You can now serve the "shell" of the site instantly because it's been added to the Service Worker cache. The HTTP request for these resources never needs to go to the server again. As soon as the user navigates to another page, they'll see the shell without delay (see figure 2.6).

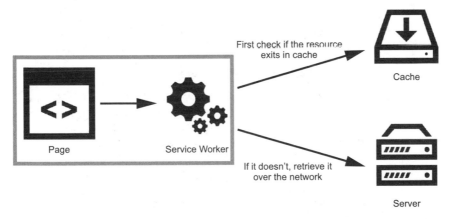

Figure 2.6 For any HTTP requests that are made, you can check whether the resource already exists in cache, and if it doesn't, retrieve it via the network.

The dynamic content that will be loaded into the site can then continue as normal. As you tap into the fetch event for these requests, you could decide at this point whether you want to cache them or not. You may have dynamic content that frequently updates, so it might not make sense to cache it. But your users will still receive a faster, enhanced browsing experience. In chapter 3, we'll dive deeper into Service Worker caching.

2.3 *Dissecting an existing PWA step by step*

Although it's a relatively new concept, some amazing PWAs are already on the web being used by millions of users every day.

In chapter 3, you'll start building your own PWA. First, let's dissect an existing PWA to see how some of these features work.

In this section, we'll look at one of my favorite PWAs, the Twitter mobile website, a PWA that offers users an enhanced experience on their mobile devices. If you use Twitter, it's a great way to view your tweets on the go (see figure 2.7).

If you navigate to twitter.com on your mobile device, you'll be redirected to mobile.twitter.com and shown a different site. Twitter named its PWA Twitter Lite, because it takes up less than a megabyte of storage, and claims it can save up to 70% on data while loading 30% faster.

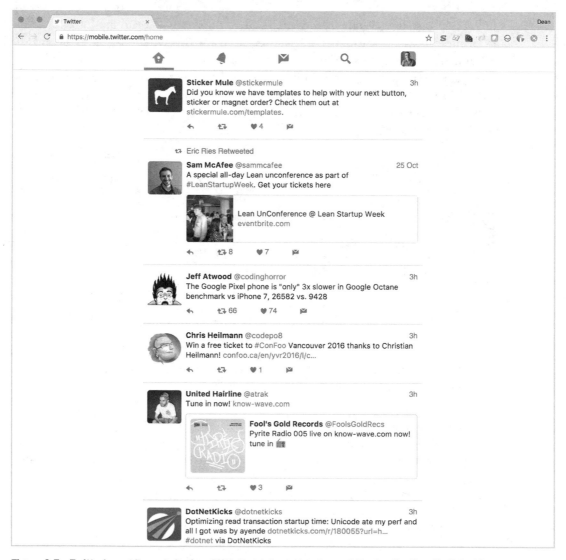

Figure 2.7   Twitter's mobile website is a PWA that takes advantage of the Application Shell Architecture.

Personally, I think it's so good that it should be used on the desktop web too. I prefer to use the PWA version over the native version—you can access the web app on your desktop device by navigating directly to mobile.twitter.com.

2.3.1 Front-end architecture

Under the hood, Twitter Lite is built using an Application Shell Architecture. This means it uses a simple HTML page for the UI shell of the site, and the main contents of the page are dynamically injected using JavaScript. If the user's browser supports Service Workers, all the assets that are needed for the UI shell are cached during the Service Worker installation.

For repeat visitors, this means that the shell loads in an instant (see figure 2.8). This approach will still work in browsers that don't support Service Workers; they won't have the assets for the UI shell cached and will miss out on the added bonus of super-fast performance. The web app has also been optimized for a range of different screen sizes using responsive web design.

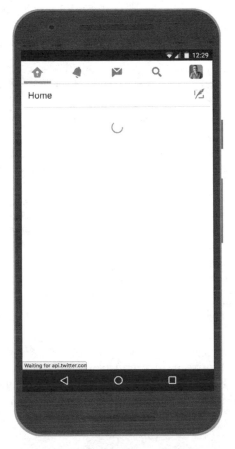
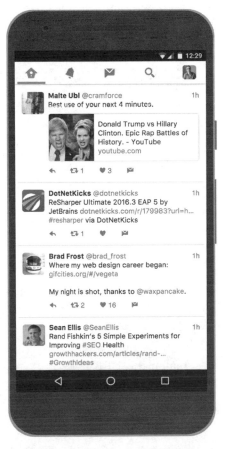

Figure 2.8   The App Shell Architecture instantly brings meaningful pixels to the screen. The image on the left is what user sees first, and then the user sees the screen on the right once it's loaded.

2.3.2 Caching

Service Worker Caching is a powerful feature that gives web developers the ability to programmatically cache the assets you need. You can intercept HTTP requests and responses and adjust them as you see fit, and this is the key to unlocking even better web applications. Using a Service Worker allows you to tap into any network requests and decide exactly how you want to respond. Building a fast and resilient PWA is easy using Service Worker caching.

Twitter Lite is fast. It feels good to use, and the pages that have been cached load almost instantly. As a user, it's the kind of experience I'd like to expect from every website.

At the time of writing this, Twitter Lite uses a handy library called the Service Worker Toolbox that contains tried and tested caching techniques using Service Workers. This toolbox provides you with a few basic helpers to get you started creating your own Service Workers and saves you from writing repetitive code. In chapter 3, we'll deep-dive into caching, and without jumping too far ahead, let's have a look at a caching example using the Service Worker Toolbox. The Twitter PWA app is using this technique to cache its emojis. Don't worry if the code in the next listing doesn't make sense right now—we'll dig deeper into this in the chapter 3.

Listing 2.1   The Twitter Lite Service Worker code

Intercept any requests for the path /emoji/v2/svg/:icon.

Open an existing cache called twemoji.

Check if the current request matches anything in your cache.

```
toolbox.router.get("/emoji/v2/svg/:icon", function(event) {
    return caches.open('twemoji').then(function(response) {
        return response.match(event.request).then(function(response) {
            return response || fetch(event.request)
        })
    }).catch(function() {
        return fetch(event.request)
    })
}, {
    origin: /abs.*\.twimg\.com$/
})
```

If it does, return that immediately. Otherwise continue as normal.

If something goes wrong when opening the cache, continue as normal.

You also only want to check for this resource against the twimg.com domain.

In listing 2.1, the Service Worker Toolbox is looking for any incoming requests that match the URL /emoji/v2/svg/ and come from an origin of *.twimg.com. Once it intercepts any HTTP requests that match this route, it will store them in cache with the name twemoji. The next time a user makes a request for the same route, they will be presented with the cached result.

This powerful snippet of code gives you as a developer the ability to control exactly how and when you want to cache assets on your site. Don't worry if that code seems a little confusing at first. In chapter 3, you'll build a page that uses this powerful feature.

2.3.3 Offline browsing

On my daily commute to and from work, I catch the train. I'm lucky that the journey isn't too long, but unfortunately the network signal is weak in some areas and can drop off. This means that if I'm browsing the web on my phone, I may lose the connection or the connection may become flaky. It can be quite frustrating.

Fortunately, Service Worker caching saves assets to the user's device. Using Service Workers, you can intercept any HTTP requests and respond directly from the device. You don't even need access to the network to retrieve cached assets.

With this in mind, you can build offline pages. Using Service Worker caching, you can cache individual resources or even entire web pages—it's up to you. For example, if the user has no connection, Twitter Lite presents a custom offline page, as shown in figure 2.9.

Instead of seeing the dreaded "This site can't be reached" error, the user now sees a helpful custom offline page or a cached version of a page they've already visited. The user can check whether connectivity has been restored by tapping the button provided. For the user, this is a better web experience. In chapter 8, you'll master the necessary skills required to start building your own offline pages and provide your users with a resilient browsing experience.

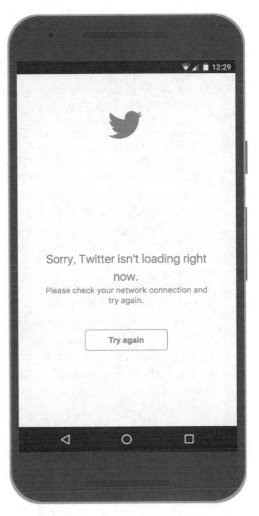

Figure 2.9 If a user has no connection, the Twitter PWA displays a custom error page.

2.3.4   Look and feel

Twitter Lite is fast, optimized for smaller screens, and works offline. What else is left? Well, it needs to look and feel like an app. If you look closely at the HTML for the home page of the web app, you might notice the following line:

```
<link rel="manifest" href="/manifest.json">
```

This link points to a file known as a manifest file. This is a simple JSON file that follows the W3C's Web App Manifest specification[1] and gives the developer control over different elements of the look and feel of the app. It provides information such as name, author, icon, and description of your web app. It gives you a few other benefits as well. First, it enables the browser to install the web application to the home screen of a device in order to provide users with quicker access and a richer experience. Also, by setting a brand color in the manifest file, you can customize the splash screen that's presented automatically by the browser. And it allows you to customize the address bar of your browser to match your brand colors.

Using a manifest file rounds off the look and feel of your web application and provides users with a richer experience. Twitter Lite uses a manifest file to take advantage of many of the features that are automatically built into the browser.

In chapter 6, we'll explore how you can use the manifest file to enhance the look and feel of your PWA and provide your users with an engaging browsing experience.

2.3.5   The final product

Twitter Lite is a well-rounded example of what a PWA should be. It covers most of the features that we'll run through in this book in order to build a fast, engaging, and reliable web application.

In chapter 1, we talked about all the features of what a web app should be. Let's review the breakdown of the Twitter PWA so far. The app can be described by all of the following:

- *Responsive*—It adjusts to smaller screen sizes.
- *Connectivity-independent*—It works offline due to Service Worker caching.
- *App-like interactions*—It's built using the Application Shell Architecture.
- *Always up-to-date*—It's updated thanks to the Service Worker update process.
- *Safe*—It works over HTTPS.
- *Discoverable*—A search engine can find it.
- *Installable*—It's installable using the manifest file.
- *Linkable*—It can be easily shared by URL.

Whoa! That's a big list—we get many of these things as side effects of building a PWA.

---

[1] www.w3.org/TR/appmanifest/

2.4   *Summary*

The features that Progressive Web Apps bring to the web enable you as a developer to build better websites that are faster, reliable, and more engaging for your users.

These features are baked into the browser, which means they also play along nicely with any libraries or frameworks that you may be familiar with. Regardless of whether you have an existing app or would like to build a new web app from scratch, you can tailor a PWA to your needs.

This chapter looked into Application Shell Architecture, an approach you can use to take advantage of Service Worker caching to provide your users with meaningful pixels instantly.

We dissected the Twitter PWA and discussed many of the features that are available in your browser right now.

Throughout the rest of this book we'll dive into each of these features one by one, and you'll learn how to build a lean, mean PWA like Twitter Lite.

Part 2

Faster web apps

If you've ever been in a hurry to get urgent information from a website, you know how frustrating it can be to wait for a web page to load. In fact, a study by Nielsen Norman Group found that a 10-second delay will often make users leave a site immediately—and even if they do stay, it's hard for them to understand what's going on, making it less likely that they'll succeed in any difficult tasks. If you're trying to build a business that's based online, you can easily lose your opportunity to convert that person into a sale. That's why it's so important to build web pages that are fast and work efficiently, regardless of the user's device.

In part 2, we'll focus on how you can use Service Workers to improve the performance of your Progressive Web Apps (PWAs). From caching techniques to alternate image formats, Service Workers are flexible enough to suit every situation.

Chapter 3 dives deep into Service Worker caching and helps you understand the different caching techniques that you can apply to your web app. We'll start with a basic caching example and expand into different caching approaches. Regardless of how the front end code of your site is written, using Service Worker caching can make a big difference to your page load times. We'll also look at some of the gotchas associated with caching, and I'll offer suggestions to help you deal with them. The chapter finishes off by briefly looking at a helpful library called Workbox that makes writing caching code easier.

In chapter 4, we'll talk about the Fetch API and see how you can use it to build faster web apps. The chapter covers a few sneaky tricks you can use to squeeze the best performance out of your site. I cover a technique for returning a lighter image format known as WebP. We'll also look at how you can tap into the Save-Data header on Android devices to reduce the overall weight of a web page.

Caching 3

Imagine you're on a train using your mobile phone to browse your favorite website. Every time the train enters an area with an unreliable network, the website takes ages to load—an all-too-familiar scene. This is where Service Worker caching comes to the rescue. Caching ensures that your website loads as efficiently as possible for repeat visitors.

This chapter starts off by looking at the basics of HTTP caching and what happens under the hood when your browser navigates to a URL. We'll also look closely at how you can use Service Worker caching to provide your users with a faster, more reliable website and how it works hand-in-hand with traditional HTTP caching. You'll learn how you can use Service Worker caching in a real-world application, including versioning and precaching resources. Finally, you'll discover one of my favorite Service Worker libraries: Workbox.

3.1 The basics of HTTP caching

Modern browsers are clever. They can interpret and understand a variety of HTTP requests and responses and are capable of storing and caching data until it's needed. I like to think of the browser's ability to cache information as the sell-by date on milk. In the same way you might keep milk in your fridge until it reaches the expiry date, browsers can cache information about a website for a set duration of time. After the data has expired, it will go and fetch the updated version. This ensures that web pages load faster and use less bandwidth.

Before we dive into Service Worker caching, let's take a step back and see how traditional HTTP caching works. Web developers have been able to use HTTP

31

caching since the introduction of HTTP/1.0 around the early 1990s.[1] HTTP caching allows the server to send the correct HTTP headers that will instruct the browser to cache the response for a certain amount of time.

A web server can take advantage of the browser's ability to cache data and use it to improve the repeat request load time. If the user visits the same page twice within one session, there's often no need to serve them a fresh version of the resources if the data hasn't changed. This way, a web server can use the `Expires` header to notify the web client that it can use the current copy of a resource until the specified "Expiry date." In turn, the browser can cache this resource and only check again for a new version when it reaches the expiry date. Figure 3.1 illustrates HTTP caching.

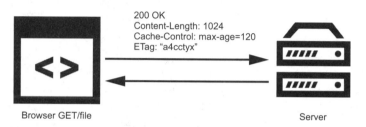

```
200 OK
Content-Length: 1024
Cache-Control: max-age=120
ETag: "a4cctyx"
```

Browser GET/file   Server

Figure 3.1   When a browser makes an HTTP request for a resource, the server sends an HTTP response containing useful information about the resource.

In figure 3.1, you can see that when a browser makes a request for a resource, the server returns the resource with a collection of HTTP headers. These headers contain useful information that the browser can then use to understand more about the resource. The HTTP response tells the browser what type of resource this is, how long to cache it for, whether it's compressed, and much more.

HTTP caching is a fantastic way to improve the performance of your website, but it isn't without flaws. Using HTTP caching means that you're relying on the server to tell you when to cache a resource and when it expires. If you have content that has dependencies, any updates can cause the expiry dates sent by the server to easily become out of sync and affect your site.

With great power comes great responsibility, and this is quite true for HTTP caching. When you make significant changes to HTML, you're likely to also change the CSS to reflect the new structure and update any JavaScript to accommodate changes to the style and content. If you've ever released changes to a website but haven't quite got your HTTP caching right, I'm sure you've seen the website break because of incorrectly cached resources.

---

[1]   https://hpbn.co/brief-history-of-http/

Figure 3.2 shows what my own personal blog looks like when I have files cached incorrectly.

As you can imagine, this can be quite frustrating for both the developer and the user. In figure 3.2, you can see that the CSS styles for the page aren't loading. That's because incorrect caching caused a mismatch.

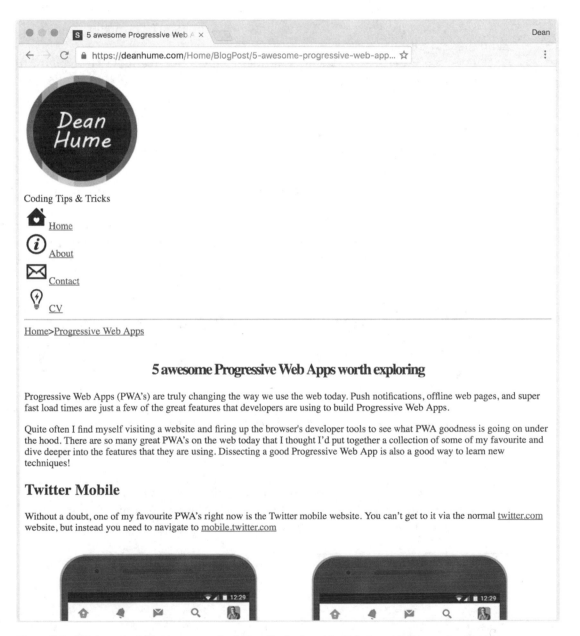

Figure 3.2   When cached files become out of sync, the look and feel of your website can be affected.

3.2   *The basics of caching Service Worker caching*

You may be wondering why you even need Service Worker caching if you have HTTP caching. How is Service Worker caching different? Well, instead of the server telling the browser how long to cache a resource, you are in complete control. Service Worker caching is extremely powerful because it gives you programmatic control over exactly how you cache your resources. As with all Progressive Web App (PWA) features, Service Worker caching is an enhancement to HTTP caching and works hand-in-hand with it.

The power of Service Workers lies in their ability to intercept HTTP requests. In this chapter, you'll use this ability to intercept HTTP requests and responses to provide users with a lightning fast response directly from cache.

3.2.1 *Precaching during Service Worker installation*

Using Service Workers, you can tap into any incoming HTTP requests and decide exactly how you want to respond. In your Service Worker, you can write logic to decide what resources you'd like to cache, what conditions need to be met, and how long to cache a resource for. You are in total control.

You may be familiar with figure 3.3—we looked at this briefly in earlier chapters of this book. When the user visits the website for the first time, the Service Worker begins downloading and installing itself. During the installation stage, you can tap into this event and prime the cache with all the critical assets for the web app.

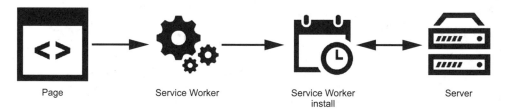

| Page | Service Worker | Service Worker install | Server |

Figure 3.3   During the Service Worker installation step, you can fetch resources and prime the cache for the next visit.

Using this figure as an example, let's see a basic caching example in order to get a better understanding about how this work in reality. The next listing shows a simple HTML page that registers a Service Worker file.

> **Listing 3.1   Simple HTML page that registers a Service Worker file**

```
<!DOCTYPE html>
<html>
  <head>
    <meta charset="UTF-8">
    <title>Hello Caching World!</title>
```

```
    </head>
    <body>
      <!-- Image -->
      <img src="/images/hello.png" />          Reference to a
      <!-- JavaScript -->                       "hello" image
      <script async src="/js/script.js"></script>   Reference to a
<script>                                               basic JavaScript file
// Register the service worker if ('serviceWorker' in navigator) {      Check to
      navigator.serviceWorker.register('/service-                       see if the
      worker.js').then(function(registration) {                         current
      // Registration was successful                                    browser
      console.log('ServiceWorker registration successful with scope: ', supports
      registration.scope);                                              Service
}).catch(function(err) {                                                Workers.
      // registration failed :(
      console.log('ServiceWorker registration failed: ', err);
      });
}
</script>                          If error during Service Worker
  </body>                          registration, you can catch it
</html>                            and respond appropriately
```

In listing 3.1, you see a simple web page that references an image and a JavaScript file. The web page isn't anything fancy, but you'll use it to learn how to cache resources using Service Worker caching. The code checks whether your browser supports Service Workers; if so, it will try to register a file called service-worker.js, assuming you're playing along at home.

We have our basic page ready. Next you need to create the code that will cache your resources. The code in the following listing goes inside the Service Worker file service-worker.js.

Listing 3.2 Code in service-worker.js

```
var cacheName = 'helloWorld';                        Name of the cache

self.addEventListener('install', event => {
  event.waitUntil(                                   Tap into the Service
    caches.open(cacheName)                           Worker install event
      .then(cache => cache.addAll([
        '/js/script.js',                             Open a cache using the
        '/images/hello.png'                          cache name we specified
      ]))
  );                                                 Add the JavaScript and
});                                                  image into the cache
```

In chapter 1, we looked at the Service Worker lifecycle and the different stages it goes through before it becomes active. One of these stages is the install event, which happens when the browser installs and registers the Service Worker. This is the perfect time to add anything into cache that you think might be used at a later stage.

For example, if you know that a specific JavaScript file might be used throughout the site, you can decide to cache it during installation. That would mean that any other pages referencing this JavaScript file will easily be able to retrieve it from cache at a later stage.

The code in listing 3.2 taps into the `install` event and adds the JavaScript file and the hello image during this stage. It also references a variable called cacheName. This is a string value that I've set to name the cache. You can name each cache differently and you can even have multiple different copies of the cache because each new string makes it unique. This will come in handy later in the chapter when we look at versioning and cache busting.

In listing 3.2, you can see that once the cache has been opened, you can then begin to add resources into it. Next you call `cache.addAll()` and pass in your array of files. The `event.waitUntil()` method uses a JavaScript promise to know how long installation takes and whether it succeeded.

If all the files are successfully cached, the Service Worker will be installed. If any of the files fails to download, the `install` step will fail. This is important because it means you need to rely on all the assets being present on the server and you need to be careful with the list of files that you decide to cache in the `install` step. Defining a long list of files will increase the chances that one file may fail to cache, leading to your Service Worker not being installed.

Now that your cache is primed and ready to go, you're able to start reading assets from it. You need to add the code in the next listing to your Service Worker in order to start listening to the fetch event.

Listing 3.3   Code to add to Service Worker to start listening to the fetch event

```
self.addEventListener('fetch', function(event) {        ◁─┐   Add an event listener
  event.respondWith(                                         to the fetch event
    caches.match(event.request)                    ◁────┐
      .then(function(response) {
        if (response) {                       ◁──┐   Check whether incoming
          return response;             ◁──┐          request URL matches anything
        }                                            that exists in the current cache
        return fetch(event.request); #E
      }                                        If there's a response and
    )                                          it isn't undefined/null,
  );                   Else continue as normal  then return it
});                    and fetch the resource
                              as intended
```

The code in listing 3.3 is the final piece of our Service Worker masterpiece. You start off by adding an event listener for the `fetch` event. Next, you check if the incoming URL matches anything that might exist in your current cache using the `caches.match()` function. If it does, return that cached resource, but if the resource doesn't exist in cache, continue as normal and fetch the requested resource.

If you open a browser that supports Service Workers and navigate to this newly created page, you should notice something similar to figure 3.4.

Figure 3.4   The sample code produces a basic web page with an image and a JavaScript file.

The requested resources should now be available in the Service Worker cache. When I refresh the page, the Service Worker will intercept the HTTP request and load the appropriate resources instantly from cache instead of making a network request to the server. In a few lines of code inside a Service Worker, you've made a site that loads directly from cache and responds instantly for repeat visits.

> **NOTE**   Service workers only work on secure origins such as HTTPS. But when you're developing Service Workers on your local machine, you can use http://localhost. Service Workers have been built this way in order to ensure safety when deployed to live, and also for flexibility, to make it easier for developers to work on their local machine.

Some modern browsers can see what's inside the Service Worker cache using the developer tools built into the browser. For example, if you open Google Chrome's Developer Tools and navigate to the Application tab, you'll see something similar to figure 3.5.

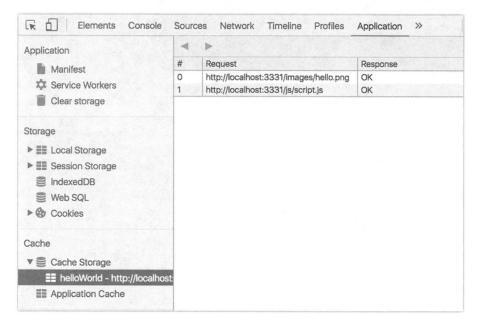

Figure 3.5   Google Chrome's Developer tools are helpful when you want to see what's stored in cache.

Figure 3.5 shows the cache entries for both the scripts.js and hello.png files stored in the cache named `helloWorld`. Now that the resources have been stored in cache, any future requests for those resources will be instantly fetched from cache.

3.2.2   *Intercept and cache*

Listing 3.2 showed how you can cache important resources during the installation of a Service Worker, which is known as precaching. This example works well when you know exactly the resources that you want to cache, but what about resources that might be dynamic or that you might not know about? For example, your website might be a sports news website that needs constant updating during a match; you won't know about those files during Service Worker installation.

Because Service Workers can intercept HTTP requests, this is the perfect opportunity to make the HTTP request and then store the response in cache. This means that instead you request the resource and then cache it immediately. That way, as the next HTTP request is made for the same resource, you can instantly fetch it out of the Service Worker cache, as shown in figure 3.6.

The next listing updates the code you previously used to include a new resource.

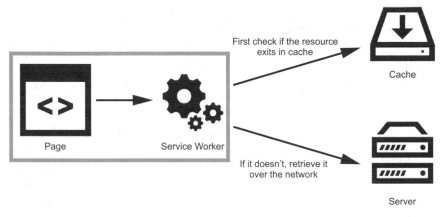

First check if the resource exits in cache

Cache

Page

Service Worker

If it doesn't, retrieve it over the network

Server

Figure 3.6   For any HTTP requests made, you can then check whether the resource already exists in cache, and if not we retrieve it via the network.

Listing 3.4   A basic web page to display Google fonts

```html
<!DOCTYPE html>
<html>
  <head>
    <meta charset="UTF-8">
    <title>Hello Caching World!</title>
    <link href="https://fonts.googleapis.com/css?family=Lato"
     rel="stylesheet">                                              ◁──┐  Add a reference
    <style>                                                              to web fonts.
    #body{ font-family: 'Lato', sans-serif; }
    </style>
</head>
  <body>
    <h1>Hello Service Worker Cache!</h1>                    JavaScript file that
    <!-- JavaScript -->                                    provides functionality
    <script async src="/js/script.js"></script>   ◁─┐     for the current page
<script>
if ('serviceWorker' in navigator) {                ◁──┤  First check whether
    navigator.serviceWorker.register('/service-           the browser supports
     worker.js').then(function(registration) {            service workers.
    console.log('ServiceWorker registration successful with scope: ',
     registration.scope);
}).catch(function(err) {                                              ◁──┐
    console.log('ServiceWorker registration failed: ', err);
    });
}
</script>                        If there is an error during the
  </body>                        service worker registration, you can
</html>                          catch it and respond appropriately.
```

In listing 3.4, the code hasn't changed much compared to listing 3.1, except that you've added a reference to web fonts in the HEAD tag. Because this is an extra resource that may be likely to change, you can cache the resource once the HTTP request has been made. You'll also notice that the JavaScript code used to register the Service Worker hasn't changed. In fact, with a few exceptions, this code is a pretty standard way of registering your Service Worker. You'll be using this boilerplate code to register a Service Worker repeatedly throughout the book.

Now that the page is complete, you're ready to start adding some code to the Service Worker file. The next listing shows the code you'll be using.

Listing 3.5 Adding code to the Service Worker file

Name of the cache →
```javascript
var cacheName = 'helloWorld';

self.addEventListener('fetch', function(event) {
  event.respondWith(
    caches.match(event.request)
      .then(function(response) {
        if (response) {
          return response;
        }

        var requestToCache = event.request.clone();

        return fetch(requestToCache).then(
          function(response) {
            if(!response || response.status !== 200) {
              return response;
            }

            var responseToCache = response.clone();

            caches.open(cacheName)
              .then(function(cache) {
                cache.put(requestToCache, responseToCache);
              });

            return response;
          }
        );
      })
  );
});
```

Annotations:
- **Add an event listener for the fetch event to intercept requests.**
- **Does the current request match anything you might have in cache?**
- **If it does, return it at this point and continue no further.**
- **Clone the request—a request is a stream and can only be consumed once.**
- **Try to make the original HTTP request as intended.**
- **If request fails or server responds with an error code, return that error immediately**
- **Again clone the response because you need to add it into cache and because it's used for the final return response.**
- **Open helloWorld cache.**
- **Add response into cache.**

Listing 3.5 seems like a lot of code. Let's break it down and explain each section. The code starts off by tapping into the fetch event by adding an event listener. The first thing you want to do is check whether the requested resource already exists in cache. If it does, you can return it at this point and go no further.

But if the requested resource doesn't already exist in the cache, you make the request as originally intended. Before the code goes any further you we need to clone the request because a request is a stream that can only be consumed once. Because you're consuming this once by cache and then again when you make the HTTP request for it, you need to clone the response at this point. You then need to check the HTTP response and ensure that the server returned a successful response and that nothing went wrong. You don't want to cache an errored result.

If the response was successful, you're clone the response again. You're probably wondering why you need to clone the response again, but remember that a response is a *stream that can only be consumed once*. Because you want the browser to consume the response as well as the cache consuming the response, you need to clone it so you have two streams.

Finally, the code then uses this response and adds it to the cache so you can use it again next time. If the user then refreshes the page or visits another page on the site that requires these resources, it will be fetched from cache instantly instead of via the network.

In figure 3.7, notice that there are new entries in the cache for the three resources on the page. In the coding example covered earlier, you were able to dynamically add a resource into cache as each successful HTTP response was returned. This technique is perfect for when you might want to cache resources but aren't quite sure how often they may change or exactly where they might be coming from.

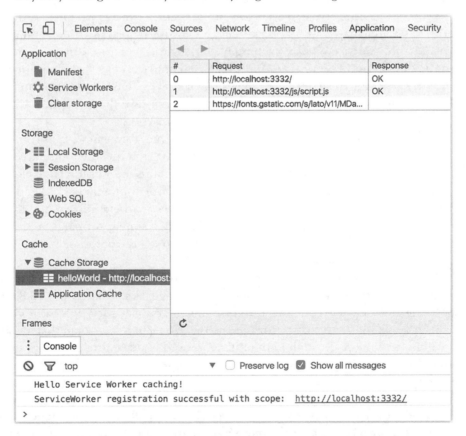

Figure 3.7 Using Google Chrome's Developer tools you see that the web fonts were retrieved from the network and then added to cache in order to ensure faster repeat requests.

Service Workers give a developer total control over the code and allow you to easily build custom caching solutions that fit your needs. In fact, the two caching techniques covered earlier can be combined to produce even faster load times. The control is in your hands.

For example, let's say you were building a new web application that used the App Shell Architecture. You might want to precache the shell using the code in listing 3.2. Then any further HTTP requests that are made can be cached using the intercept and cache technique. Or perhaps you want to cache parts of an existing site that you know don't change often. By intercepting and caching these resources, you'll provide your users with improved performance in a few lines of code. Depending on your situation, Service Worker caching can be adapted to suit your needs and make an instant difference to the experience your users receive.

3.2.3   *Putting it all together*

The code examples we've run through so far have been helpful, but it isn't easy to imagine them on their own. In chapter 1, we talked about the many different ways that you could use Service Workers to build amazing web apps. One of those concepts was a newspaper web app, which we can use to play with everything you've learned about Service Worker caching in a real-world scenario. I'm going to call our sample application Progressive Times. The web app is a news site where people will regularly visit and read multiple pages, so it makes sense to cache future pages ahead of time so they load instantly. You could even save the content so that a user could browse while offline.

The sample web application contains a collection of funny news facts from around the world (figure 3.8). Believe it or not, all the stories in this news site are true and came from credible news sources. The web app contains most of the basic elements of a website that you can imagine, such as CSS, JavaScript, and images. To keep the sample code basic, I've also used a flat JSON file for each article; in real life, this would point to a back-end endpoint to retrieve the data in a similar format. On its own, this web app is not that impressive, but when you start to use the power of Service Workers, you can take it to the next level.

The web application uses the App Shell Architecture to dynamically fetch the contents of each article and inject the data onto the page, as shown in figure 3.8.

Using the App Shell Architecture also means you can use precaching to ensure that the web app loads instantly for repeat visits. You can also assume that a visitor will tap a link and follow through to the full contents of a news article. If you cached this when the Service Worker was installed, it would mean that the next page would load significantly faster for them.

Let's put everything you learned this far in the chapter together and see how to add a Service Worker to the Progressive Times app that will precache important resources and cache any other requests as they are made, as shown in the next listing.

Empty Shell without content   Shell populated with content

Figure 3.8 **The Progressive Times sample application uses the App Shell Architecture.**

Listing 3.6 **Service Worker code to precache and Ccche resources during runtime**

```
var cacheName = 'latestNews-v1';

// Cache our known resources during install
self.addEventListener('install', event => {
  event.waitUntil(
    caches.open(cacheName)
    .then(cache => cache.addAll([
      './js/main.js',
      './js/article.js',
      './images/newspaper.svg',
      './css/site.css',
      './data/latest.json',
      './data/data-1.json',
      './article.html',
      './index.html'
    ]))
  );
});
```

◁ **Open the cache and store an array of resources to cache during install time.**

```
// Cache any new resources as they are fetched        ◄─┤  Listen for the
self.addEventListener('fetch', event => {                   fetch event.
  event.respondWith(
    caches.match(event.request, { ignoreSearch: true })  ◄─  Ignore any querystring
    .then(function(response) {                                parameters so you
      if (response) {                                         don't get any cache
        return response;                           ◄─         misses.
      }
      var requestToCache = event.request.clone();

      return fetch(requestToCache).then(           ◄─┤  If you found a successful
        function(response) {                            match, return it at this
          if(!response || response.status !== 200) {    point and go no further.
            return response;
          }                                        If you didn't find
                                                   anything in cache,
          var responseToCache = response.clone();  make the request
          caches.open(cacheName)
          .then(function(cache) {
            cache.put(requestToCache, responseToCache);  ◄─┤  Store it in cache
          });                                                so we won't need
                                                             to make that
          return response;                                  request again
        });
    })
  );
});
```

The code in listing 3.6 is a combination of precaching during install time and storing in cache as you fetch a resource. The web app is using an App Shell Architecture, which means you can take advantage of Service Worker caching to request only the data needed to populate the page. You've already successfully stored the assets for the shell, so all that's left is the dynamic news content from the server.

If you'd like to see this web page in action, it's available on GitHub and can be easily accessed at bit.ly/chapter-pwa-3. In fact, I've added all the code samples that you'll use throughout this book to that GitHub repo.

Each chapter has a readme file that explains what you need to do to start building and experimenting with the sample code in each chapter. About 90% of the chapters are front-end code, so all you need to do is fire up your localhost and get started. It's also worth noting that you need to be running the code on http://localhost environment and not on file:// environment.

3.3   *Performance comparison: before and after caching*

At this point, I hope I've managed to convince you how great Service Worker caching is. Not yet!? Okay, well, hopefully the performance improvements you'll gain when using caching will change your mind.

Using our Progressive Times sample application, we can compare the difference with and without Service Worker caching. One of my favorite ways to test the real-world performance of a website is to use a tool called WebPagetest.org, shown in figure 3.9.

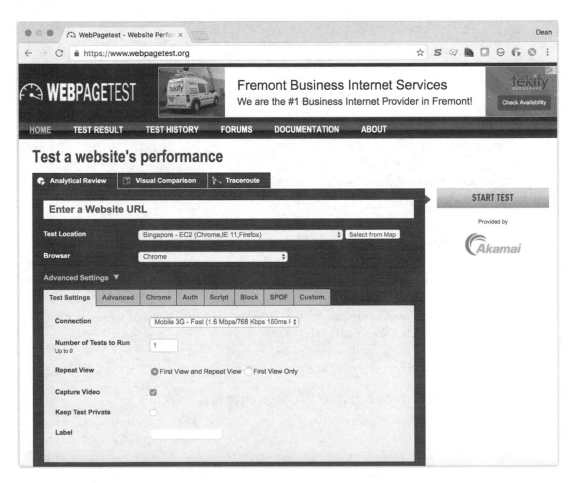

Figure 3.9   WebPagetest.org is a free tool you can use to test your websites using real devices from around the world.

WebPagetest.org is a great tool. Enter the URL of your website, and it allows you to profile your website from any location around the world using a real-world device and a wide range of browsers. The tests run on real devices and provide you with a helpful breakdown and profile of the performance of your website. Best of all, it's open source and completely free to use.

If I run our sample application through WebPagetest.org, it produces something similar to figure 3.7.

To test how our sample web application performed on a real-world device, I used WebPagetest with a 2G mobile connection from an endpoint in Singapore. If you've ever tried to access a website over a slow network connection, you'll know how annoying it can be while you wait for the site to finish loading. As web developers, it's important that we test our websites as our users would use them, and that includes using slower mobile connection speeds and low-end devices, too. Once WebpPagetest completed profiling the web app, it produced the results shown in figure 3.10.

	Load Time	First Byte	Start Render	Speed Index	Document Complete		
					Time	Requests	Bytes In
First View	12.258s	3.752s	7.481s	8030	12.258s	13	91 KB
Repeat View	0.578s	3.498s	0.476s	492	0.578s	0	0 KB

Figure 3.10   WebPagetest.org produces useful information about the performance of your web application by using a real device.

In the first view, the page took around 12 seconds to load. This isn't ideal, but not unexpected over a slow 2G connection. But if you look at the repeat view, the site loaded in less than 0.5 seconds and made zero HTTP requests to the server. The sample application used the App Shell Architecture, and if you remember the layout, you'll know that any future requests will be served as quickly because the resources needed have already been cached. If used correctly, Service Worker caching significantly improves the overall speed of your application and enhances the browsing experience regardless of the device or connection used.

3.4 *Diving deeper into Service Worker caching*

In this chapter, we've started to look at how Service Worker caching can be used to improve the performance of your web application. As we progress through the rest of this chapter, we'll look closely at how you can version your files in order to ensure that there are no cache mismatches, as well as to avoid some of the common gotchas you might encounter while using Service Worker caching.

3.4.1 *Versioning your files*

There will be a point in time where your Service Worker cache will need updating. If you make changes to your web application, be sure users receive the newer version of files instead of older versions. As you can imagine, serving older files by mistake would cause havoc on a site.

The great thing about Service Workers is that each time you make any changes to the Service Worker file itself, it automatically triggers the Service Worker update flow. In chapter 1, we looked at the Service Worker lifecycle. Remember that when a user navigates to your site, the browser tries to re-download the Service Worker in the background. If there's even a byte's difference in the Service Worker file compared to what it currently has, it considers it new.

This useful functionality gives you the perfect opportunity to update your cache with new files. You can use two approaches when updating the cache. First, you can update the name of the cache that you use to store against. Referring back to the code in listing 3.2, you can see the cacheName variable with a value 'helloWorld'. If you updated this value to 'helloWorld-2', that would automatically create a new cache and start serving your files from that cache. The original cache would be orphaned and no longer used.

The second option, which I personally feel is the more bulletproof one, is to version your files. This technique is known as *cache busting* and has been around for many years. When a static file gets cached, it can be stored for long periods of time before it ends up expiring. That can be an annoyance in the event that you make an update to a site, but because the cached version of the file is stored in your visitors' browsers, they may be unable to see the changes made. Cache busting solves this problem by using a unique file version identifier to tell the browser that a new version of the file is available.

For example, if you were to add a reference to a JavaScript file in the HTML, you might want to append a hashed string onto the end of the filename, similar to this:

```
<script type="text/javascript" src="/js/main-xtvbas65.js"></script>
```

The idea behind cache busting is that you create a completely new filename each time you make changes to the file in order to ensure that the browser fetches the freshest content possible. Imagine the following scenario in our newspaper web app. Let's say you have a file called main.js and store it in cache exactly as it is. Depending on how your Service Worker is set up, it will retrieve this version of the file from cache every time. If you make a change to the main.js file with new code, the Service Worker will still intercept and return the older cached version even though you want to serve the newer version of the file. But if you rename the file to, say, main.v2.js and update your code to point to this new version, you can ensure that the browser will get the fresh version every time. That way, your newspaper will always return the freshest results to your users.

There are many different approaches to implementing this solution, and all of them may depend on your coding environment. Some developers prefer to generate these hashed filenames during build time, and others may do this using code and generate the filenames on the fly. Whichever approach you use, this technique is a tried-and-tested way to ensure that you always serve the correct files.

3.4.2 Dealing with extra query parameters

When a Service Worker checks for a cached response, it uses a request URL as the key. By default, the request URL must exactly match the URL used to store the cached response, including any query parameters in the search portion of the URL.

If you make any HTTP requests for files appended with query strings that sometimes change, this might end up causing you a few issues. For example, if you make a request for a URL that previously matched, you may find that it misses because the query string differs slightly. To ignore query strings when you check the cache, use the ignoreSearch attribute and set the value to true, as shown in the following listing.

Listing 3.7   Service Worker code to ignore query string parameters

```
self.addEventListener('fetch', function(event) {
  event.respondWith(
    caches.match(event.request, {
      ignoreSearch: true
    }).then(function(response) {
      return response || fetch(event.request);
    })
  );
});
```

The code in listing 3.7 uses the ignoreSearch option to ignore the search portion of the URL in both the request argument and cached requests. You can extend this further by using other ignore options such as ignoreMethod and ignoreVary. For example, the ignoreMethod value will ignore the method of the request argument, so a POST request can match a GET entry in the cache. The ignoreVary value will ignore the vary header in cached responses.

3.4.3   *How much memory do you need?*

Whenever I talk to developers about Service Worker caching, the questions that regularly arise involve memory and storage space. How much space does the Service Worker use to cache? How will this memory usage affect my device?

The honest answer is that it depends on your device and storage conditions. Like all browser storage, the browser is free to throw it away if the device comes under storage pressure. That's not necessarily a problem because the data can then be fetched again from the network as needed. In chapter 7, we'll look at another type of storage called *persistent storage* that can be used to store cached data on a more permanent basis.

Right now, older browsers are still able to store cached responses in their memory, and the space they use isn't different from the space that the Service Worker uses to cache resources. The only difference is that Service Worker caching puts you in the driving seat and allows you to programmatically create, update, and delete cached entries, allowing you to access resources without a network connection.

3.4.4   *Taking caching to the next level: Workbox*

If you find yourself regularly writing code in your Service Workers that caches resources, you might find Workbox (https://workboxjs.org/) helpful. Written by the team at Google, it's a library of helpers to get you started creating your own Service Workers in no time, with built-in handlers to cover the most common network strategies. In a few lines of code, you can decide whether you want to serve specific resources solely from cache, serve resources from cache and then fall back, or perhaps only return resources from the network and never cache. This library gives you total control over your caching strategy. See figure 3.11.

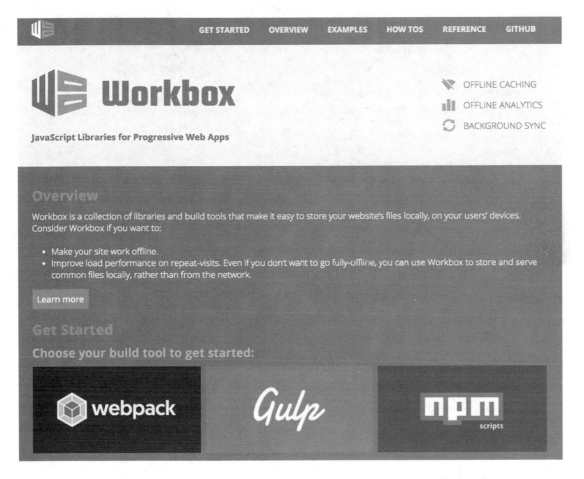

Figure 3.11   Workbox provides a library of helpers for use in creating your own Service Workers.

Workbox provides you with a quick and easy way to reuse common network caching strategies instead of rewriting them again and again. For example, say you wanted to ensure that you always retrieve your CSS files from the cache but only fall back to the network if a resource wasn't available. Using Workbox, you register your Service Worker the same way you have throughout this chapter. Then you import the library into your Service Worker file and start defining routes that you want to cache.

In listing 3.8, the code starts off by importing the Workbox library using the importScripts function. Service Workers have access to a global function, called importScripts(), which lets them import scripts in the same domain into their scope. This is a handy way to load another script into an existing script. It keeps the code clean and means you only load the file when it's needed.

Listing 3.8   Using Workbox

```
importScripts('workbox-sw.prod.v1.1.0.js');        ◄─┐  Load the
                                                       Workbox library.
const workboxSW = new self.WorkboxSW();

workboxSW.router.registerRoute(                    ◄─┐  Start caching any
  'https://test.org/css/(.*)',                         requests that match
  workboxSW.strategies.cacheFirst()                    the '/css' path.
);
```

Once the script has been imported, you can start defining routes you want to cache. In listing 3.8, you're defining a route for anything that matches the '/css/' path and always serving it with a cache first approach. This means that the resources will always be served from cache and will fall back to the network if they don't exist. Workbox also provides a number of other built-in caching strategies,[2] such as cache only, network only, network first, cache first, or fastest, which tries to find the fastest response from either cache or the network. Each of these strategies can be applied to different scenarios, and you can even mix and match them with different routes to achieve the best effect.

Workbox also provides you with functionality to precache resources. In the same way that you precached resources during installation of the Service Worker in listing 3.2, you can achieve this with a few lines of code using Workbox.

Whenever I approach a new project, without a doubt my favorite library to use is Workbox. It simplifies your code and provides you with tried-and-tested caching strategies that you can implement in a few lines of code. In fact, the Twitter PWA we dissected in chapter 2 uses Workbox to make the code simpler to understand and relies on these tried-and-tested caching approaches.

3.5   *Summary*

HTTP caching is a fantastic way to improve the performance of your website, but it isn't without flaws.

Service Worker caching is extremely powerful because it gives you programmatic control over exactly how you cache your resources. When used hand-in-hand with HTTP caching, you get the best of both worlds.

Used correctly, Service Worker caching is a massive performance enhancement and bandwidth saver.

You can use a number of different approaches to cache resources, and each of them can be adapted to suit the needs of your users.

WebPagetest is a great tool for testing the performance of your web apps using real-world devices.

Workbox is a handy library that provides you with tried-and-tested caching techniques.

---

[2] www.recode.net/2016/6/8/11883518/app-boom-over-snapchat-uber

Intercepting
network requests

4

Chapter 3 looked into using Service Worker caching to dramatically speed up the performance of your website. Instead of the user making a request to the server, the Service Worker intercepts the request and decides to serve it from cache instead. We also briefly touched on how to use Service Workers to transform the requests and responses made by the client using the fetch event.

In this chapter, we'll dive deeper into the fetch event and you'll learn more about the many use cases it offers. Service Workers are the key to unlocking the power that lies within your browser. By the end of the chapter, you'll know how to serve lighter, leaner web pages depending on your user's browser or preferences. In this section of the book, we're focusing on the *faster* part of Progressive Web Apps (PWAs), although it's important to also ensure that your web apps are resilient and engaging, too.

4.1   The Fetch API

As web developers, we often need the ability to retrieve data from the server in order to update our applications asynchronously. Traditionally, this data is retrieved using JavaScript and the XMLHttpRequest object. Otherwise known as AJAX, this is a developer's dream because it allows you to update a web page without reloading the page by making HTTP requests in the background. In our sample application, Progressive Times, you use this code to retrieve a list of news articles.

If you've ever implemented complex logic to retrieve data from the server, writing code using the XMLHttpRequest object can be quite tricky. As you start to add more and more logic and callbacks, it can quickly become messy, as you can see in the following listing.

Listing 4.1   HTTP eequest using the `XMLHTTPRequest` **object**

```
var request;
if (window.XMLHttpRequest) {
    request = new XMLHttpRequest();
} else if (window.ActiveXObject) {
    try {
        request = new ActiveXObject('Msxml2.XMLHTTP');
    } catch (e) {
        try {
            request = new ActiveXObject('Microsoft.XMLHTTP');
        } catch (e) {}
    }
}

request.onreadystatechange = function() {
    if (this.readyState == 4 && this.status == 200) {
        doSomething(this.responseText);
    }
  };

// Open, send.
request.open('GET', '/some/url', true);
request.send();
```

The code in listing 4.1 seems like a lot of code to make an HTTP request. The interesting thing is that the `XMLHttpRequest` object was originally created by the developers of Outlook Web Access for Microsoft Exchange Server. After a number of permutations, it eventually became the standard for what we use today to make HTTP requests in JavaScript. The example in the listing fulfills its purpose, but it isn't as clean as it could be. The other problem with the code in the listing is that the more complex your logic becomes, the more complex this code will become. In the past, a number of libraries and techniques were available to make this code simpler and easier to read, with popular libraries such as jQuery and Zepto, including cleaner APIs.

Fortunately, modern browser vendors have realized that this situation needed to be updated, and this is where the Fetch API comes in. The Fetch API is a part of the Service Worker global scope, and you can use it to make HTTP requests inside any Service Worker. Up until now, you've been using the Fetch API inside your Service Worker code, but we haven't dived deeper into it. Let's look at a few code examples in order to get a better understanding of the Fetch API, beginning with the following listing.

Listing 4.2   An HTTP Request Using the Fetch API

```
fetch('/some/url', {                          ◁──      The URL to access
    method: 'GET'                                      using a GET request
}).then(function(response) {      ◁──
    // success                                   If successful, return
}).catch(function(err) {          ◁──            the response.
    // something went wrong
});                                              If something went wrong, you
                                                 can respond appropriately.
```

The code in listing 4.2 is a basic example of the Fetch API in action. You might also notice that there are no callbacks and events—they've been replaced with the then() method. This method is part of ES6's new promises functionality and aims to make your code much more readable and easier for developers to understand. A *promise* represents the eventual result of an asynchronous operation, even if the value won't be known until the operation completes at some point in the future.

Listing 4.2 seems easy enough to understand, but what about a POST request using the fetch API? Check out the next listing.

Listing 4.3 An HTTP POST request using the Fetch API

```
fetch('/some/url', {                              ◁      The URL to access
        method: 'POST',                                   using a POST request
        headers: {
          'auth': '1234'
        },                                        ◁      Headers can be included
         body: JSON.stringify({          ◁              in the request.
        name: 'dean',
        login: 'dean123',                         The body of the
      })                                          POST request
   })
   .then(function (data) {                 ◁      If successful, return
     console.log('Request success: ', data);       the response.
   })
   .catch(function (error)                   ◁      If something went
     console.log('Request failure: ', error);       wrong, you can respond
   });                                              appropriately.
```

Say you wanted to send some user details to the server and needed to do so using a POST request. In listing 4.3, you change the method to POST and add a body parameter in the fetch options. Not only does using promises make your code cleaner, it also allows you to chain code together to share logic across fetch requests.

The Fetch API is currently available in all browsers that support Service Workers, but if you intend to use this API on browsers that aren't supported, you may want to consider using a polyfill. A *polyfill* is a piece of code that provides you with the functionality you expect from a modern browser. For example, if the latest version of Internet Explorer has some functionality you need, but it doesn't exist in an older version, you can use a polyfill to provide similar functionality for the older browser. Think of it as a wrapper around an API that's used to keep the API landscape flattened. A polyfill written by the team at GitHub (https://github.com/github/fetch) will ensure that older browsers are able to make requests using the Fetch API. Include it in your web page and you'll be able to start writing code using this API.

4.2 *The fetch event*

A Service Worker's ability to intercept any outgoing HTTP requests is what makes it so powerful. Every HTTP request that falls within this service worker's scope will trigger this event—for example, HTML pages, scripts, images, CSS, and so on. This gives you as a developer total control over how you want to handle the way the browser responds to any of these `fetches`.

In chapter 1, we looked at a basic example of the `fetch` event in action. Remember the unicorn (shown in the next listing)?

Listing 4.4   The `fetch` event inside a Service Worker

```
self.addEventListener('fetch', function(event) {          ◁──┐  Add an event listener
  if (/\.jpg$/.test(event.request.url)) {     ◁──────────────┘  to the fetch event.
    event.respondWith(
      fetch('/images/unicorn.jpg'));     ◁──┐
  }                                         │  Check to see whether
});                Try to fetch an image of │  the HTTP request URL
                   a unicorn and respond    │  requests a file ending in .jpg.
                   with it instead.
```

In listing 4.4, you're listening out for the `fetch` event, and if the HTTP request is for a JPEG file, you're intercepting it and forcing it to return a picture of a unicorn instead of its original intended URL. The code here will do this for each and every HTTP request made for a JPEG file from the website. For any other file types, it will ignore them and move on.

Although the code in listing 4.4 is a fun example, it doesn't show you what Service Workers are capable of. Let's take this a step further and see how to return your own custom HTTP response, as shown in the following listing.

Listing 4.5   Creating a custom HTTP response inside a Service Worker

```
                                                      Add an event listener
                                                      to the fetch event.
self.addEventListener('fetch', function(event) {   ◁──┘
  if (/\.jpg$/.test(event.request.url)) {                        ◁──────┐
    event.respondWith(
    new Response('<p>This is a response that comes from your service
    worker!</p>', {
      headers: { 'Content-Type': 'text/html' }    ◁──┐              Check to see
      });                                            │          whether the HTTP
    );                                    Build a custom          request URL
  }                                     Response and respond      requests a file
});                                       accordingly.            ending in .jpg.
```

In listing 4.5, the code intercepts any HTTP requests by listening for the fetch event to be triggered. Next it determines if the incoming request is for a JPEG file, and if it is, it will respond with a custom HTTP response. Using Service Workers, you can build your own custom HTTP responses, including editing their headers. This functionality makes Service Workers extremely powerful—which is why you can understand that they need to serve requests over HTTPS. Imagine the malicious things a hacker could get up to with this at their fingertips.

4.2.1 *The Service Worker lifecycle*

Right at the beginning of the book in chapter 1, you learned about the Service Worker lifecycle and the role it plays when building PWAs. Let's look closely at that diagram again in figure 4.1.

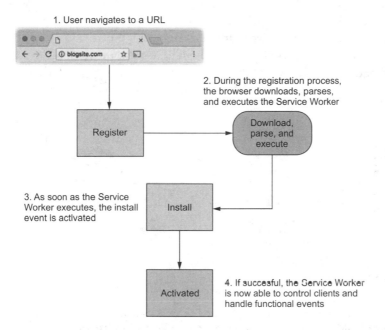

Figure 4.1   Lifecycle of a Service Worker

Looking at figure 4.1, you'll remember that when a user visits your website for the first time, they don't have an active Service Worker controlling the page. Only once the Service Worker has been installed and they refresh the page, or navigate to another part of the site, does the Service Worker become active and start intercepting requests.

To explain this more clearly, imagine a Single Page Application (SPA) or a web page with AJAX interactions that might take place after a page has been loaded. When you register and install a Service Worker using the method you've been using in the book up until now, any HTTP requests that take place after the page has loaded will be missed. Only when the user reloads the page will the Service Worker become active and start intercepting requests. This isn't ideal because ultimately you want the Service Worker to start working its magic as soon as possible and include these requests that are made while the Service Worker isn't active.

If you want your Service Worker to start working immediately instead of waiting for the user to navigate to another part of your site or reload the page, there's a sneaky little trick that you can use to activate your Service Worker immediately, shown in the following listing.

Listing 4.6 Install the current Service Worker without waiting for reload

```
self.addEventListener('install', function(event) {
  event.waitUntil(self.skipWaiting());
});
```

The code in listing 4.6 sits inside the `install` event of your Service Worker. By using the `skipWaiting()` function, you're ultimately triggering the `activate` event and telling the Service Worker to start working immediately without waiting for the user to navigate or reload the page.

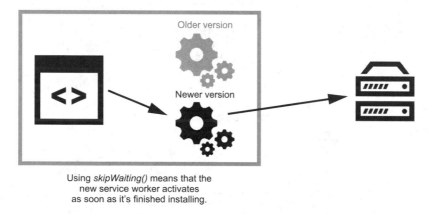

Using *skipWaiting()* means that the
new service worker activates
as soon as it's finished installing.

Figure 4.2 `self.skipWaiting()` **causes your Service Worker to kick out the current active worker and activate itself as soon as it enters the waiting phase.**

The `skipWaiting()` function forces the waiting Service Worker to become the active Service Worker. The `self.skipWaiting()` function can also be used with the `self.clients.claim()` function to ensure that updates to the underlying Service Worker take effect immediately.

The code in the next listing can be combined with the `skipWaiting()` function in order to ensure that your Service Worker activates itself immediately.

Listing 4.7 Activate a Service Worker immediately

```
self.addEventListener('activate', function(event) {
  event.waitUntil(self.clients.claim());
});
```

The code in listings 4.6 and 4.7 can be used together to kick-start the activation of your Service Worker. If your site has complex AJAX requests taking place once the page has loaded, these functions are perfect. If your site serves mostly static pages without HTTP requests taking place once the page has loaded, you may not need to use these functions.

4.3   *Fetch in action*

As we've seen in this chapter, Service Workers offer almost unlimited control of the network. Intercepting HTTP requests, editing HTTP responses, and crafting your own responses are a small part of what you can do by tapping into the `fetch` event.

Up until now, most of the code samples we've looked at haven't been real-world examples. In the next section, we're going to dive in to two useful techniques you can use to make your website faster, more engaging, and resilient.

4.3.1   *An example using WebP images*

Images play an important role on the web today. Imagine a world without images on our web pages. High-quality images can make a website stand out, but unfortunately they come with a price. Due to their large file sizes, they're bulky to download and result in slow page load times. If you've ever been on a device with a poor network connection, you'll know how frustrating this experience can be.

You may be familiar with the image format WebP. Developed by the team at Google, WebP files are 26% smaller than PNG images and around 25–34% smaller than JPEG images. That's a pretty decent savings, and the best thing about them is that the image quality isn't noticeably affected when choosing this format, as you can see in figure 4.3.

Original image   WebP image

Figure 4.3   WebP images are significantly smaller in file size compared to their original format with little noticeable difference to the quality of the image.

Figure 4.3 shows a WebP image next to its equivalent JPEG image with negligible difference to image quality. By default, WebP images are supported in Chrome, Opera, and Android, but unfortunately not by Safari, Firefox, or Internet Explorer.

Browsers that support WebP images notify you of that fact by passing through an `accept: image/webp` header with each HTTP request. Given that you have Service Workers at your disposal, this seems like a perfect opportunity to start intercepting requests and returning lighter, leaner images to browsers that can render them.

The basic web page in the following listing references an image of Brooklyn Bridge in New York.

Listing 4.8   A basic HTML web page including a JPEG image

```
<!DOCTYPE html>
<html>
 <head>
  <meta charset="UTF-8">
  <title>Brooklyn Bridge - New York City</title>
 </head>
 <body>
<h1>Brooklyn Bridge</h1>
<img src="./images/brooklyn.jpg" alt="Brooklyn Bridge - New York">
      <script>
          // Register the service worker
          if ('serviceWorker' in navigator) {
          navigator.serviceWorker.register('./service-
    worker.js').then(function(registration) {
 // Registration was successful
console.log('ServiceWorker registration successful with scope: ',
    registration.scope);
          }).catch(function(err) {
            // registration failed :(
              console.log('ServiceWorker registration failed: ', err);
          });
          }
      </script>
 </body>
</html>
```

That image is in JPEG format and comes in at 137 KB. If you convert it to WebP and store it on the server, you can choose to return this for browsers that support it and fall back to the original for those that don't.

The next listing shows code in your Service Worker that you can use to start intercepting the HTTP request for this image.

Listing 4.9   Service Worker Code to Return WebP Images if the Browser Supports It

```
"use strict";

// Listen to fetch events
self.addEventListener('fetch', function(event) {      Check whether the
                                                      incoming request is
  if (/\.jpg$|.png$/.test(event.request.url)) {       for an image of type
                                                      JPEG or PNG.
    var supportsWebp = false;
    if (event.request.headers.has('accept')) {        Inspect the accept header
      supportsWebp = event.request.headers            for WebP support.
```

```
        .get('accept')
        .includes('webp');
    }
    if (supportsWebp) {
        var req = event.request.clone();

        var returnUrl = req.url.substr(0, req.url.lastIndexOf(".")) + ".webp";

        event.respondWith(
            fetch(returnUrl, {
                mode: 'no-cors'
            })
        );
    }
  }
});
```

Does the browser support WebP?

Build the return URL.

There's a lot of code going on in listing 4.9. Let's step back and break it down further. In the first few lines, you're adding an event listener to listen out for any `fetch` events that take place. For each HTTP request that takes place, you check to see whether the current request is for a JPEG or PNG image. If you know the current request is for an image, you can then determine the best content to return based on the HTTP headers that are passed through. In this case, you're inspecting each header and looking for the `image/webp` mime type. Once you know the header values, you can determine whether the browser supports WebP images and return the corresponding WebP image.

Once the Service Worker has activated and is ready, any requests for a JPEG or PNG image will be returned as its WebP equivalent for any browsers that support it. If the browser doesn't support WebP images, it won't advertise the support in the HTTP request header, and the Service Worker will ignore the request and work as normal.

The WebP equivalent comes in at 87 KB, and compared to its JPEG equivalent, you've managed to save 59 KB—around 37% of the original file size. For users on a mobile device, this could add up to a big bandwidth saver across your site.

Service Workers open up a world of endless possibilities, and this example could be extended to include other image formats, and even caching. You could easily add support for Internet Explorer's improved image format called JPEGXR. There's no reason why you can't reward your users with fast web pages right now.

4.3.2 An example using the Save-Data header

I was recently travelling abroad when I urgently needed to get some information from my airline's website. I was on a sketchy 2G connection that took forever to load the page and eventually I gave up completely. I was also paying a fortune for this daily service from my mobile provider back home—so frustrating!

4G-network coverage is rapidly accelerating worldwide, but there's still a long way to go. 3G networks were only launched in late 2007 in countries such as Bangladesh, Brazil, China, India, Nigeria, Pakistan, and Russia—where almost 50% of the global population is located.[1] Although mobile coverage is growing, it's crazy to think that a 500 MB data plan can cost around 17 hours' worth of minimum wage work in India.[2]

Fortunately, browser vendors such as Google Chrome, Opera, and Yandex have realized the pain that many users face. With the latest versions of these browsers, users can opt-in to a feature that will save them data. Once this feature is enabled, the browser will add a new header to each HTTP request. Developers can look out for this header and return the appropriate content to save users data. For example, if a user has opted-in to save data, you could return lighter images, smaller videos, or even different markup. It's a simple concept, but effective.

This sounds like a perfect situation to use a Service Worker. In the next section, you'll build code that will intercept whether or not a user has opted-in to save data and return a lighter version of your PWA.

Remember the PWA you built in chapter 3? Called Progressive Times, it contains a collection of funny news facts from around the world (figure 4.4).

Figure 4.4   The Progressive Times sample application is a basic app we'll revisit throughout the book.

---

[1] https://gsmaintelligence.com/research/2014/12/mobile-broadband-reach-expanding-globally/453
[2] http://blog.jana.com/2015/05/21/the-data-trap-affordable-smartphones-expensive-data

In the Progressive Times app, you're using web fonts to improve the look and feel of the app.

These fonts are downloaded from a third-party service and come in at around 30 KB. Web fonts do enhance the look and feel of a web page, but if users are trying to save data and money at the same time, web fonts seem unnecessary. There's no reason why your PWA can't cater to users regardless of their network connection.

Whether you're on a desktop or mobile device, enabling this feature is a relatively straightforward process. If you're on a mobile device, you can enable this under the Settings in your menu, as shown in figure 4.5.

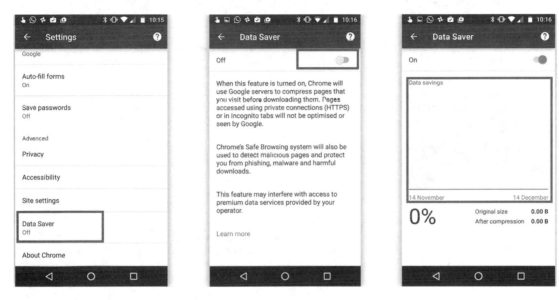

Figure 4.5   You can enable the Save-Data feature on your mobile device or on a phone. Note the highlighted areas in red.

Once the setting is enabled, each HTTP request to the server will include the Save-Data header. If you view this using your developer tools, it might look a little something like figure 4.5.

Once the Save-Data feature has been enabled, you can use a few different techniques to return data to the user. Because each HTTP request will go to the server, you could decide to serve different content based on the Save-Data header directly from server-side code. But with a few lines of JavaScript and using the power of Service Workers, you could easily intercept the HTTP requests and serve lighter content accordingly. If you're developing a front-end application that's API-driven and don't have access to the server, this is a perfect option.

Service Workers allow you to intercept outgoing HTTP requests, inspect them, and act on this information. Using the Fetch API, you can easily implement a solution to detect the Save-Data header and serve lighter content.

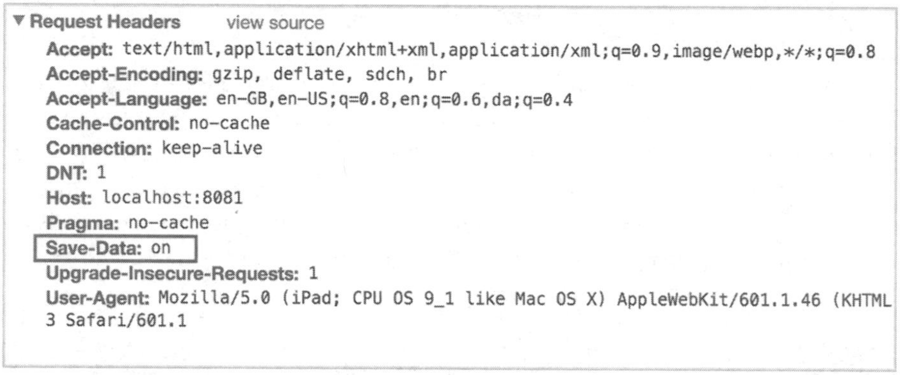

```
▼ Request Headers      view source
    Accept: text/html,application/xhtml+xml,application/xml;q=0.9,image/webp,*/*;q=0.8
    Accept-Encoding: gzip, deflate, sdch, br
    Accept-Language: en-GB,en-US;q=0.8,en;q=0.6,da;q=0.4
    Cache-Control: no-cache
    Connection: keep-alive
    DNT: 1
    Host: localhost:8081
    Pragma: no-cache
    Save-Data: on
    Upgrade-Insecure-Requests: 1
    User-Agent: Mozilla/5.0 (iPad; CPU OS 9_1 like Mac OS X) AppleWebKit/601.1.46 (KHTML
    3 Safari/601.1
```

Figure 4.6   With the Save-Data feature enabled, each HTTP request will include this in the header.

You'll get started by creating a JavaScript file called service-worker.js and adding the code in listing 4.10 to it.

Listing 4.10   Service Worker code to check for the save-data HTTP header

```
"use strict";

this.addEventListener('fetch', function (event) {

  if(event.request.headers.get('save-data')){
    // We want to save data, so restrict icons and fonts
    if (event.request.url.includes('fonts.googleapis.com')) {
        // return nothing
        event.respondWith(new Response('', {status: 417, statusText: 'Ignore
    fonts to save data.' }));
    }
  }
});
```

Based on the examples we've looked at already, the code in listing 4.10 should look familiar. In the first few lines, you're adding an event listener to listen out for any `fetch` events that take place. For each request that takes place, you're inspecting the header and checking to see if the Save-Data header has been enabled. If it has been, you then check to see if the current HTTP request is for a web font from the domain fonts.googleapis.com. Because you're looking to save your users unnecessary data, you return a custom HTTP response with a 417-status code and your own custom status text. HTTP status codes provide users with specific information from the server;[3] in the case of a 417 status code, it's "The server cannot meet the requirements of the Expect request-header field."

---

[3] https://en.wikipedia.org/wiki/List_of_HTTP_status_codes

Using this simple technique and a few lines of code, you were able to reduce the overall download size of the page and ensure that the user saved on any unnecessary data. You could extend this technique further and return images of a lower quality, or other larger downloads on your site.

You can see any of the code in this chapter in action on GitHub at http://bit.ly/ chapter-pwa-4.

4.4 Summary

The Fetch API is a new browser API that aims to make your code cleaner and easier to read.

The fetch event allows you to intercept any outgoing HTTP requests to and from your browser. This functionality is extremely powerful and allows you to alter responses or even create your own custom HTTP responses without even hitting the server.

WebP images are 26% smaller in file size than PNG images and around 25–34% smaller in file size than JPEG images.

Using Service Workers, you can tap into the fetch event and intercept if the browser supports WebP images. Using this technique, you can serve smaller images to your users and speed up your page load times.

Some modern browsers have an opt-in to a feature that allows users to save data. If the feature is enabled, the browser adds a new header to each HTTP request. Using Service Workers you can tap into the fetch event and decide if you want to return a lighter version of your site.

Part 3

Engaging web apps

As many failed startups will testify, having a great web app just isn't enough these days. Our users expect great software that's easily accessible. The unfortunate truth is that if your software isn't meeting their increased expectations, they'll seek out other options. Although it's important to build websites that are fast, it's even more important to build websites that engage your users and keep them coming back for more. This part of this book focuses on just that: building engaging Progressive Web Apps (PWAs) using the features that are already built into your browser.

In chapter 5, we'll explore a few different ways to enhance the look and feel of your PWA, including the Add to Homescreen functionality and customization. This chapter looks at the web manifest file and the role it plays in PWAs. You'll also learn about customizing your web apps icons, the splash screen, and the different launch styles available.

Chapter 6 focuses on one of my favorite features: web push notifications. You'll discover why push notifications can increase engagement with your users and learn how to apply them to your own web app. We'll build a working example that sends push notifications using the sample application Progressive Times. Finally, you'll learn about the different types of push notifications and how you can build interactivity into them.

By the end of this part, you'll know how to begin building your own PWAs that are truly engaging and that harness the power that already lies within the browser.

Look and feel

5

Up until this point in the book, we've focused on key features that make up a Progressive Web App (PWA). To create truly engaging applications that delight your users, you need to focus on your PWA's visual appeal. In this chapter, we'll explore a few different ways to enhance the look and feel of your PWA including the Add to Home Screen functionality and customization, which prompts users to add your web app to their home screen.

5.1   *The web app manifest*

A *web app manifest* file is a simple JSON file that provides useful information about the application (such as its name, author, icon, and description) in a text file. But more specifically, the web app manifest enables a user to install web applications to the home screen of their device and allows you to customize the splash screen, theme colors, and even the URL that's opened.

But before all that, it's time to code! Using our sample Progressive Times application, the following listing adds a basic web app manifest file (a manifest.json file) to it.

Listing 5.1   Web app manifest file

```
{
  "name": "Progressive Times web app",
  "short_name": "Progressive Times",
  "start_url": "/index.html",
  "display": "standalone",
  "theme_color": "#FFDF00",
  "background_color": "#FFDF00",
```

```
  "icons": [
    {
      "src": "homescreen.png",
      "sizes": "192x192",
      "type": "image/png"
    },
    {
      "src": "homescreen-144.png",
      "sizes": "144x144",
      "type": "image/png"
    }
  ]
}
```

The code in listing 5.1 is a basic web app manifest that tells the browser a lot about the current website. Each field in the file plays a role and tells the browser how your PWA will look and feel:

- name is used as the text that appears when the user is prompted to install the app.
- short_name is used as the text that appears on the user's home screen when the app is installed.
- start_url determines the first page that appears when a user opens the web app from the home screen of their device. We'll look into this more later in the chapter.
- Depending on the type of web application you are building, you may want to preset how it's first loaded. The display field represents how developers would like their web application to appear to a user. We'll dive deeper into why this field is important later in the chapter.
- By using the theme_color field, you can color the address bar of the browser to match your site's primary colors.
- The icons field determines the icons to use when the web app is added to the home screen on the device.

Before we break down the manifest file any further, you'll reference it in your Progressive Times app and see how it looks. To reference a manifest file, you'll need to add a link tag to all the pages in your web app. The code in the next listing shows a web app manifest file that's referenced using a link tag between the head tags of a web page.

Listing 5.2   Linking to a web app manifest file in an HTML file

```
<!DOCTYPE html>
<html>
  <head>
    <meta charset="UTF-8">
    <title>Progressive Times</title>
    <link rel="manifest" href="/manifest.json">       <--┐   The web app manifest
  </head>                                                    file is referenced
                                                             between the head tags
                                                             in a web page.
```

```
<body>
..content goes here..
</body>
</html>
```

Now that the manifest file has been referenced in your sample application, the browser is able to determine how it should behave under certain circumstances.

In our manifest file (the code in listing 5.1), we told the browser to use the hex color #FFDF00 as the theme_color throughout the site. As you can tell from figure 5.1, the address bar has been styled to match the color we chose.

Using a web app manifest to style your web app is one piece of the puzzle—it can provide so much more functionality. Let's take this a step further and look at how the web app manifest file is used to provide the Add to Home Screen functionality on your device.

5.2   Add to Home Screen

When I need quick access to an application on the go, it's so easy to open up my home screen and tap an icon and it opens immediately. This sort of behavior is the default for native apps on your device. As web developers, if we want to engage our users and keep them coming back for more, we need the same functionality.

Figure 5.1   The theme_color property in the web app manifest can be used to style your web app.

This is where the Add to Home Screen feature comes in.

Add to Home Screen, also known as a web app install banner, is a great way to quickly and seamlessly allow your users to add your web app to their home screens without ever leaving the browser. In order to ensure that your users can quickly access your website, this functionality displays a prompt asking the user whether or not they want to add your web app to their home screen, as shown in figure 5.2. If they accept, an icon is added to the home screen of their device that references the URL of your application. This makes accessing your web app only a tap away.

In chapter 1, we looked at a company in India called Flipkart and discussed how they built a PWA called Flipkart Lite. Flipkart wanted their mobile web users to enjoy the same, if not a better, experience than their native application users. By using the Add to Home Screen functionality, 60% of all visits to Flipkart Lite come from people launching the site from the home screen icon. This functionality has meant that their

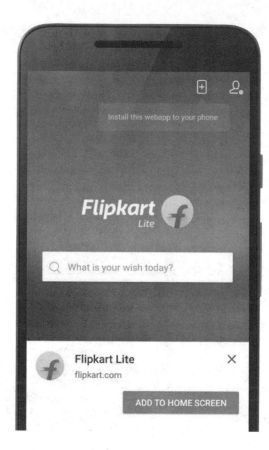

**Figure 5.2   The Add to Home Screen
functionality is a great way to engage
with your users and keep them coming
back for more.**

customers convert 70% more from viewers to buyers than people who stumbled on the site.[1] These two activities alone resulted in engagement numbers that were 40% higher than before.

In figure 5.3, you can see the different steps that take place when a user is prompted with the Add to Home Screen banner. When a user visits the site under the right conditions, they will be prompted with the banner. If they accept, an icon will be added to their home screen and will be easily accessible the next time that they wish to visit the site.

From a developer's point of view, the best thing about the Add to Home Screen functionality is that you have to write almost zero code to get the banners to appear; the browser will do most of the heavy lifting for you.

---

[1] https://developers.google.com/web/showcase/2016/flipkart

Figure 5.3 **With the correct code in place, your users will be prompted to add your web app to their home screen.**

Here are the criteria that need to be met before the Add to Home Screen prompt will be shown:

- You need a manifest.json file.
- Your manifest file needs a start URL.
- You need a 144 x 144 PNG icon.
- Your site must be using a Service Worker running over HTTPS.
- The user must have visited your site at least twice, with at least five minutes between visits.

Of those criteria, the last one is perhaps the most important. The reason that the prompt will only appear after the user has visited the site at least twice with at least five minutes between visits is to ensure that this feature doesn't become annoying and spammy. Imagine if every site that visited used this technology and the Add to Home Screen prompt appeared on every page. It would quickly become annoying, and browser vendors would find themselves in hot water.

This functionality is also built into the browser, which means you have no control over the criteria just mentioned. As we progress through this chapter, you'll learn different techniques that give you fine-tuned control over when and how the prompt appears.

5.2.1 *Customizing the icons*

When a user is prompted to add your web app to their home screen and they accept, the first thing they'll see is your icon on their home screen. This is easily added to your manifest.json file, as shown in the next listing.

Listing 5.3

```
"icons": [
    {
      "src": "homescreen.png",
      "sizes": "144x144",
      "type": "image/png"
    }
  ]
```

In listing 5.3, I've shortened the code in the manifest file to only display the icons section for brevity. You're allowed to provide a list of different icons of different sizes in the icons array that can be used in various contexts and displayed differently depending on the device. For example, they can be used to represent the web application among a list of other applications, or to integrate the web application with an OS's task switcher and/or system preferences. Figure 5.4 shows this in action.

Figure 5.4 Customizing your web app using the manifest file means it integrates with the operating system in order to provide a truly app-like feel.

In our sample application, Progressive Times, I've added a manifest file and referenced an icon that I want to appear when it's installed on the home screen. You can find all the code at bit.ly/chapter-pwa-5. Once installed, the icon should appear on the home screen of a user's device and look similar to figure 5.5.

Figure 5.5 The icon that will appear on the home screen matches the icon in the web app manifest file.

5.2.2 Add a splash screen

When a user taps the icon of your web application on their home screen, they see a temporary splash screen while the browser renders the first frame of the document. The splash screen is designed to improve the perceived performance of the loading of your site and can help make a user feel as if your site loaded a little bit faster than it did. With your manifest file in place, most of this functionality comes for free.

The following listing provides the basic code that you need.

Listing 5.4 Web app manifest file using background color for the splash screen

```
"name": "Progressive Times web app",
"theme_color": "#FFDF00",
"background_color": "#FFDF00",
```

The name and background_color properties are used to display the splash screen.

```
"icons": [
  {
    "src": "homescreen.png",
    "sizes": "192x192",
    "type": "image/png"
  }
]
```

The splash screen is generated dynamically from information held in the manifest file. It uses a combination of the name and background_color properties, and the icon in the icons array that the browser chooses to be most suitable based on dimensions.

Using the code in listing 5.4, you should notice a splash screen similar to figure 5.6.

5.2.3 *Set the launch style and URL*

In order to add the final cherry on top of your Add to Home Screen functionality, you'll need to set a display mode and start URL. The *display mode* determines how you want your web app to appear on the user's device, and the *start URL* is the first page that a user will land on when they've tapped the home screen icon.

Both of these values are defined in your manifest file, as shown in the next listing.

Figure 5.6   The splash screen uses a combination of the name and background_color properties to style how it will look.

Listing 5.5   Web app manifest file using display mode to set launch style

```
"start_url": "/index.html",
 "display": "standalone",
```

In listing 5.5, the start URL is used to specify the URL that loads when a user launches the application from a device. If given as a relative URL, the base URL will be the URL of the manifest. If you want to track how many people arrive on your website via the home screen icon, you may want to append a tracking code in a query string, such as `/index.html?homescreen=1`, to the URL too. This way, your web analytics package will be able to determine users arriving via the home screen icon.

You have a few different options when it comes to how you want your web app to appear on your user's device. For example, you can choose the display mode that best suits your needs using the display value. A display mode represents how the web application is being presented within the context of an OS: `fullscreen`, `standalone`, `minimal-ui`, or `browser`.

Each of these display modes has the following effects on your web app:

- fullscreen—Opens the web application and takes up the entirety of the available display area.
- standalone—Opens the web application to look and feel like a standalone native application. In this mode, the user agent will exclude standard browser UI elements such as a URL bar, but might include other system UI elements such as a status bar and/or system back button.
- minimal-ui—This mode is similar to fullscreen, but provides the user with access to a minimal set of UI elements—for example, the back button, forward button, reload button, and perhaps some way of viewing the document's address.
- browser—Opens the web application using the standard browser built into the OS.

In your web app manifest, the display property is optional and by default it will display in normal browser mode. These different display modes open up a world of possibilities for developers, so you should think about how you want your web app to appear. For example, if your web app is a game, it might make sense to use the standalone display mode in order to make the web app feel more immersive. If your web app is an online publication, you might choose the minimal-ui or fullscreen display mode in order to focus on the text and remove clutter. This control is in your hands, but remember: whichever style you choose will have an influence on how your web app is perceived, so choose wisely.

5.3 Advanced Add to Home Screen usage

The Add to Home Screen functionality allows your users to keep coming back for more at the tap of a finger. The fact that this functionality is built into the browser natively is great for us as developers, but it does mean that most of this functionality is controlled by the browser.

There may be occasions where you want to override the default settings and provide your own logic, such as cancelling or deferring the Add to Home Screen banner altogether. Fortunately, there are ways to use code to control certain behaviors.

5.3.1 Cancelling the prompt

If for some reason you'd prefer not to show the Add to Home Screen banner, you can cancel it completely, as shown in the next listing. Depending on which type of web app you have, it may not make sense to show this prompt. Perhaps your site covers sensitive topics or a short-lived event for which the banner might be more annoying to the user than helpful.

Listing 5.6 Preventing the Add to Home Screen Banner from appearing

```
window.addEventListener('beforeinstallprompt', function(e) {
  e.preventDefault();
  return false;
});
```

The code in listing 5.7 will listen for the beforeinstallprompt event and prevent the default behavior of the banner if it's fired. The code is straightforward and uses the standard JavaScript preventDefault() functionality to cancel the event and returns a false value—both of which are needed to ensure that the banner doesn't appear.

5.3.2 Determining usage

The Add to Home Screen functionality can be helpful for your users, but it's important to find out if it would be or not. Are your users annoyed by the banner and dismiss it when it appears? Do they trust your application enough to add it to their device?

By listening for the beforeinstallprompt event, you can determine whether a user decided to add your web app to their home screen or if they dismissed it. The following listing shows how.

> **Listing 5.7 Tracking whether a user accepted or fismissed the A2HS banner**

```
window.addEventListener('beforeinstallprompt', function(event) {
  event.userChoice.then(function(result) {          ◁──┐  Determine the user's choice
                                                         - returned as a Promise
    console.log(result.outcome);

    if(result.outcome == 'dismissed') {             ◁──  Based on the user's choice,
      // Send to analytics                                decide how to proceed
    }
    else {
      // Send to analytics
    }
  });
});
```

In listing 5.8, I've added an event listener to the beforeinstallprompt event. This event has an object called userChoice that returns a promise with the user's decision. You can then use the result of this promise to determine whether the user dismissed or confirmed the prompt.

At this point, you could decide to send this information to your Web Analytics tools to track the usage of this functionality over time. This technique can be a useful approach for understanding how your users interact with your Add to Home Screen prompt.

5.3.3 Deferring the prompt

Using a combination of the code in listings 5.7 and 5.8, you can defer the Add to Home Screen banner to appear until a later time—for example, if a user visits a site and has met the criteria for the banner to be shown, but you'd prefer them to add your site by allowing them to tap a custom button on your site instead. This puts the user in control of whether or not they'd like to add your site, instead of the browser choosing when it should show the banner.

The code in the next listing is for a basic web page with a button that shows the prompt when clicked.

Listing 5.8 Basic HTML page that displays the A2HS banner when a button is tapped

```
<!DOCTYPE html>
<html>
  <head>
    <meta charset="UTF-8">
    <title>Progressive Times</title>                          This button shows
  </head>                                                      the prompt.
  <body>
    <button id="btnSave" disabled>Click this to show the prompt</button>
  </body>
<script>
    window.addEventListener('load', function() {

      var btnSave = document.getElementById('btnSave');
      var savedPrompt;

      if ('serviceWorker' in navigator) {            Check if Service
                                                     Workers are supported
    navigator.serviceWorker.register('/service-      and register if they are.
    worker.js').then(function(registration) {
        // Registration was successful
        console.log('ServiceWorker registration successful with scope: ',
    registration.scope);
      }).catch(function(err) {

        // Registration failed :(
          console.log('ServiceWorker registration failed: ', err);
        });
      }

      window.addEventListener('beforeinstallprompt', function(e) {

        e.preventDefault();                          Add an event listener to the
                                                     beforeinstallprompt event.
        btnSave.removeAttribute('disabled');

        savedPrompt = e;                             Stash the event in a
                                                     variable so it can be
        return false;                                triggered later.
      });

      btnSave.addEventListener('click', function() {    Add an event listener
        if (savedPrompt !== undefined) {                to the click event of
          savedPrompt.prompt();                         the button.

          savedPrompt.userChoice.then(function(result) {   Follow what
                                                           the user has
            if (result.outcome == 'dismissed') {           selected.
```

At this point you can enable the button.

User has had a positive interaction with our app, and Chrome has tried to prompt previously, so show the prompt.

```
                console.log('User dismissed homescreen install');
              }
              else {
                console.log('User added to homescreen');
              }

              savedPrompt = null;                ◁──┐  You no longer
          });                                          need the prompt,
        }                                              so clear it.
      });
    });
  </script>

</html>
```

There's a lot going on in listing 5.9. Let's break it down. The code is a simple web page that registers a Service Worker. Remember that one of the criteria for the Add to Home Screen functionality is that the page has an active Service Worker working over HTTPS. Next, the code contains an event listener that's fired when the before-installprompt event takes place. When this event is fired, the code prevents the banner from being shown and saves the event object in a variable named saved-Prompt.

Now that you have this event saved in another variable, you can allow the user to show the Add to Home Screen prompt when they tap the button. Using the code in listing 5.8, you've successfully deferred the Add to Home Screen functionality and given the user control over when they'd like to see the prompt appear.

5.4   *Debugging your manifest file*

In this chapter, we've looked at how you can use the web app manifest file to control the appearance of your app as well as customize the splash screen, theme colors, and even the URL that's opened when a user adds your app to their home screen. The web app manifest is a simple JSON file, but due to its being text-based, making a mistake and typing incorrect values is easy. Fortunately, you have a few different options for debugging your web app manifest and ensuring that you have the correct values.

Using both Google Chrome and Opera, you are able to see the different values in a helpful visual display. If you open up either Google Chrome or Opera and fire up the Developer Tools, you should see a tab called Applications. If you choose Manifest, you will be presented with something similar to figure 5.7.

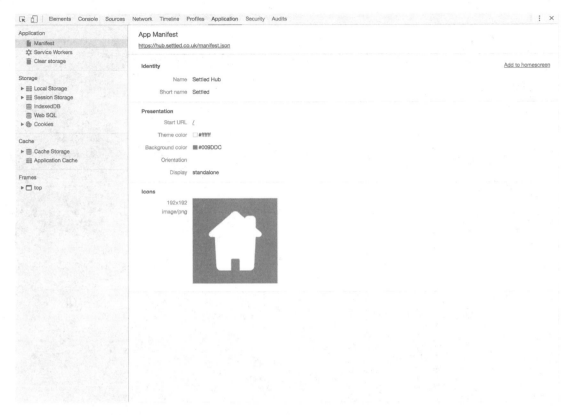

Figure 5.7   Both Google Chrome and Opera have tools built into their Developer Tools that are helpful for visualizing the values in your web app manifest file.

The Developer Tools in both Opera and Google's Chrome provide you with a quick and useful way to see the different values in your web app manifest and adjust accordingly.

If you'd prefer to parse the contents of your web app manifest file and instead find out if there are any major issues with it, navigate to manifest-validator.appspot.com in your browser and you'll be able to either provide the validator with a URL or paste the contents of a web app manifest and have it validated.

The web app manifest validator (figure 5.8) checks the file and uses the W3C specification to determine whether it's valid. If you're having trouble understanding why your web app manifest doesn't seem right, the tool will provide you with feedback about which character caused an issue and also suggest different reasons that could be causing the issue.

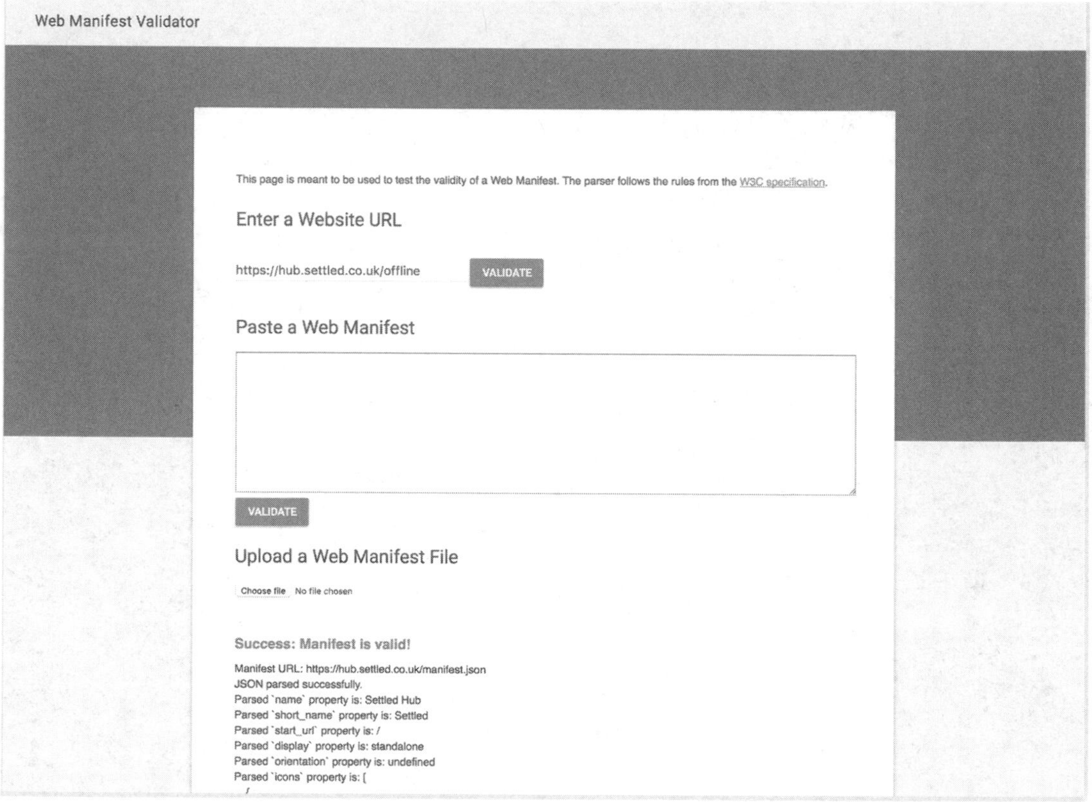

Figure 5.8   The manifest validator is a useful tool when debugging your web app manifest file.

5.5   *Summary*

A web app manifest file is a simple JSON file that lets you control how your web app appears to your users. It provides useful information about the application (such as its name, author, icon, and description) in a text file.

Add to Home Screen, also known as a web app install banner, is a great way to quickly and seamlessly allow your users to add your web app to their home screens without leaving the browser.

Using the web app manifest file, you can control various settings such as the icons, splash screen, and start URL of your web app.

Using JavaScript code, you can control various behaviors of the Add to Home Screen functionality, such as canceling the prompt completely or deferring it until later.

The Developer Tools in both Opera and Google's Chrome provide you with a quick and useful way to see the different values in your web app manifest and adjust accordingly.

Using a tool like the manifest validator can be useful when debugging your web app manifest file.

Push notifications 6

You've released your amazing Progressive Web App (PWA) to your customers and you're looking for a way to keep them engaged and up-to-date on your site. Where do you turn? Email? In-app notifications? Believe it or not, push notifications could be the perfect solution. In this chapter, you'll discover the basics of push notifications and why they can increase engagement with your users. You'll build a working example that sends push notifications using the sample application, Progressive Times. Once you've run through the steps in this chapter, you'll be able to implement your own push notifications in no time.

6.1 Engaging with your users

Most modern web apps need the ability to update and communicate with their users on a regular basis. Communication channels such as social media, emails, and in-app notifications are great, but they don't always grab the attention of the user, especially when the user navigates away from the website.

This is where push notifications come in. They're those helpful notifications that appear on your device that prompt you about information that could be useful to you. You can swipe or tap away to close them, or you can tap them and be instantly directed to a web page with the relevant information. Traditionally, only native applications had this amazing ability to tap into the operating system of a device and send push notifications. This is where PWAs are a game changer. They have the ability to receive push notifications that appear in the browser, as the example in figure 6.1 shows.

Figure 6.1   Push notifications can be a great way to engage with your users when they close the tab or navigate away.

The best thing about push notifications is that the user receives them even when they aren't browsing your site. The experience looks and feels like a native app and works even if the browser isn't running. This makes it a perfect way to engage with users and draw them back to your web app even if they haven't opened the browser in a while. For example, if your website is a weather application, a push notification could provide your users with useful information such as warnings about approaching bad weather. You could even schedule weekly weather forecasts that can be sent as a push notification, depending on how your users subscribe. The possibilities are endless.

But what about malicious websites using this technology to send spammy push notifications? In order to send push messages to a user, the user first needs to opt in to your messages. Whenever they visit your web app for the first time, they're presented with a prompt that looks similar to figure 6.2.

Once a user has either accepted or blocked the push notification prompt, the prompt won't appear again. It's important to note that that this prompt will only appear if the site is running over HTTPS, has a registered Service Worker, and you have written code for it.

Mobile

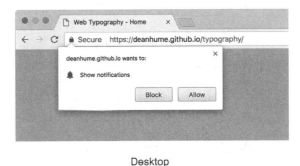

Desktop

Figure 6.2   A user will be prompted on their device to choose whether they want to opt into receiving push notifications.

6.2   *Engagement insight: The Weather Channel*

The Weather Channel has been forecasting since the 1980s and now serves people all around the world across many platforms. Weather is volatile, and delivering important data when people need it isn't always easy, so the team was interested in improving its mobile web experience.

Around half of the Weather Channel's traffic is from people accessing its site via the web on their mobile devices. For the Weather Channel, the mobile web is also an extremely important discovery portal in markets where users don't have the latest smartphones or reliable connectivity, or where there's significant cost for downloading a native app.

To scale their development quickly, the Weather Channel decided to implement push notifications for the web before creating a full blown PWA, as shown in figure 6.3. Within three months, they noticed impressive results. The Weather Channel saw almost 1 million users opt in to receive web push notifications, with 52 percent coming from mobile.[1] The Weather Channel has a global audience, so being able to provide

---

[1]   https://developers.google.com/web/showcase/2016/pdfs/weather-channel.pdf

a PWA experience with the most reliable weather information to people across the world in their local language has been key in growing that user base. On a technical level, they made this efficient by enabling support for over 60 languages using one code base.

The Weather Channel is one of many organizations out there benefitting from web push notifications. Sending your first web push notification is also easier than you think, so let's get started.

6.3   *Browser support*

At the time of writing this book, the Push API is supported by the major browsers Firefox, Chrome, and Opera, with Microsoft's Edge support currently in development. Safari does have support for web notifications, but it doesn't use the Push API and Service Workers. If you would like to target Safari too, I recommend checking out the Safari developer's website (https://developer.apple.com/notifications/safari-push-notifications/) for more information.

Figure 6.3   The Weather Channel used push notifications to increase engagement across their web presence.

All the code we've covered in this chapter is based on a web push standard (www.w3.org/TR/push-api/), which means that when you write it once, it will work on all browsers that follow this standard.

6.4   *Your first push notification*

In this next section, we're going to break down all the pieces required to start sending and receiving notifications. Figure 6.4 shows how all the pieces fit together.

First, the browser displays a prompt asking a user if they'd like to opt in to notifications. If they accept, you can save their subscription details on the server and use them to send notifications later. These subscription details are unique to each user, device, and browser, so if a user logs in to your site on multiple devices, they'll be prompted once per device.

Once they've accepted, you can use these stored subscription details to send messages to a user later with a scheduled task that updates users with timely information.

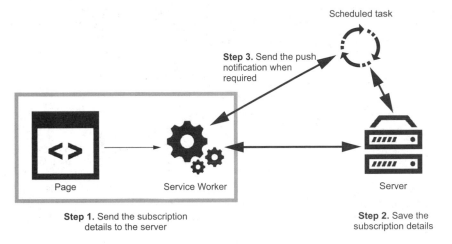

Figure 6.4 Sending push notifications requires a three-step approach: prompt the user and get their subscription details, save these details on the server, and send any messages when required.

Using the Weather Channel as an example, a scheduled task could be used to send daily information about the weather forecast for a certain region. It could also be used to send a tornado alert or warning about dangerous weather approaching.

As we progress through this chapter, we'll look at both server-side and client-side code. Most of the coding examples in this book have been using JavaScript, which is why I've chosen to use Node.js for the server-side code too. If you aren't familiar with Node.js, don't worry—these code listings serve as examples, which means you can use any server-side language you like. By the end of the chapter you'll be sending your own messages with ease.

When you think about web push notifications and the moving parts involved, it all can seem quite daunting. I'll break each step down slowly so you can see how all the parts of the jigsaw puzzle fit together, enabling you to subscribe a user and start sending them web push notifications.

6.4.1   *Subscribing to notifications*

Before you can start sending notifications to a user, you need to ask their permission by displaying a prompt. This prompt functionality is built into the browser by default, but first you need to add a little code to ensure that this prompt is initiated. If a user accepts the prompt, you'll be provided with a subscription object containing information about their subscription. But if a user denies the prompt, you won't be able to send them any messages, and they won't be prompted again. This ensures that you aren't able to annoyingly prompt users every time they visit your site.

The code in the following listing shows a web page that registers a Service Worker.

Listing 6.1   A web page with code to subscribe a user to push notifications

```
<!DOCTYPE html>
<html>
  <head>
    <meta charset="UTF-8">
    <title>Progressive Times</title>
    <link rel="manifest" href="/manifest.json">
  </head>
  <body>
  <script>
  var endpoint;
  var key;
  var authSecret;
var vapidPublicKey =
    'BAyb_WgaR0L0pODaR7wWkxJi__tWbM1MPBymyRDFEGjtDCWeRYS9EF7yGoCHLdHJi6hikYd
    g4MuYaK0XoD0qnoY';

  function urlBase64ToUint8Array(base64String) {
    const padding = '='.repeat((4 - base64String.length % 4) % 4);
    const base64 = (base64String + padding)
      .replace(/\-/g, '+')
      .replace(/_/g, '/');

    const rawData = window.atob(base64);
    const outputArray = new Uint8Array(rawData.length);

    for (let i = 0; i < rawData.length; ++i) {
      outputArray[i] = rawData.charCodeAt(i);
    }
    return outputArray;
  }

  if ('serviceWorker' in navigator) {
    navigator.serviceWorker.register('sw.js').then(function(registration) {
        return registration.pushManager.getSubscription()
          .then(function(subscription) {

            if (subscription) {
                return;
            }

            return registration.pushManager.subscribe({
                userVisibleOnly: true,
                applicationServerKey: urlBase64ToUint8Array(vapidPublicKey)
            })
              .then(function(subscription) {

                var rawKey = subscription.getKey ?
        subscription.getKey('p256dh') : '';
                key = rawKey ? btoa(String.fromCharCode.apply(null, new
        Uint8Array(rawKey))) : '';
                var rawAuthSecret = subscription.getKey ?
        subscription.getKey('auth') : '';
                authSecret = rawAuthSecret ?
```

> A web app manifest file is referenced in the HEAD tag.

> A public key is needed on both the front end and server to ensure the message is encrypted.

> Convert VAPID key from base64 string to Uint8 Array because VAPID specification requires this.

> Get any existing subscriptions.

> They already have a subscription; you don't need to register them again.

> They don't have a subscription, so get the prompt to appear.

> Get the key and authSecret from the subscription object.

```
                btoa(String.fromCharCode.apply(null, new
    Uint8Array(rawAuthSecret))) : '';

                endpoint = subscription.endpoint;

                return fetch('./register', {
                    method: 'post',
                    headers: new Headers({
                        'content-type': 'application/json'
                    }),
                    body: JSON.stringify({
                        endpoint: subscription.endpoint,
                        key: key,
                        authSecret: authSecret,
                    }),
                });
            });
        });
    }).catch(function(err) {
    // registration failed :(
    console.log('ServiceWorker registration failed: ', err);
    });
}

</script>
</body>
</html>
```

Send the details through to the server to register the user.

The code in listing 6.1 seems a little tricky, so let's step through each function. You start off by referencing a web app manifest file in the HEAD tag of the HTML page. Toward the bottom of the page, you have a SCRIPT tag with the code you need to start sending web push notifications.

In order to send push notifications, you need to use the VAPID protocol.[2] *VAPID* is short for Voluntary Application Server Identification. It's a specification that defines a handshake between your app server and the push service and allows the push service to confirm which site is sending messages. This is important because it means that an application server is able to include additional information about itself that can be used to contact the operator of the application server. Having a standard like VAPID in place is a great step forward, because it means that ultimately all browsers will conform to a single standard, allowing web push to work seamlessly for you as a developer, regardless of browser.

In listing 6.1 there's a VAPID public key that needs to be included in the subscription details sent to the server. Both the front-end code and the server contain this public key. Don't worry about this key too much for now—we'll look at how to generate one when we dive into the server-side code.

Next you may notice code you've used frequently throughout this book. You register the Service Worker and, if it's successful, you can then use the registration object

---

[2] https://tools.ietf.org/html/draft-thomson-webpush-vapid-02

to determine whether the user has any existing subscriptions by inspecting the push-Manager object. If the user is already subscribed on this machine, you don't need to send the information to the server again. Remember that each subscription object contains a subscription ID that's unique to a given machine. This is useful for user privacy because you won't know anything about the user, but rather only a unique ID.

If the user isn't already subscribed, you prompt them to subscribe using the push-Manager.subscribe() function, which uses the VAPID public key to identify itself. Before you prompt the user, you need to include the VAPID public key and ensure that it's been converted to a UInt8Array. It needs to be sent through as a UInt8Array because the specification only accepts this type. If a user accepts the web push prompt in the browser, the subscribe function returns a promise containing the subscription object. From this object, you can then extract the key and the authSecret that you need to use to send through to the server when subscribing them.

Finally, you use the Fetch API to POST through the endpoint on the server, the key, and the authSecret that will be used to store the user's details and send messages to them at a later date.

6.4.2   Sending notifications

In order to keep the server-side code as easy to follow as possible, I'm using a Node.js server that can receive the user's subscription details and send push messages using the web push protocol. The server uses Express, which is a minimalist web framework for Node.js. If this is your first time looking at code written for a Node.js server, note that it's still written in JavaScript, which should hopefully make the transition easier.

The server-side code in the next listing creates an endpoint that listens to POST requests that are directed to '/register'. This code will be used to save the user's subscription details as well as to send them a thank-you message.

Listing 6.2   Sending push notification from a Node.js application

```
const webpush = require('web-push');              Add the required
const express = require('express');               dependencies.
var bodyParser = require('body-parser');
const app = express();

webpush.setVapidDetails(                     Set the VAPID details.
  'mailto:contact@deanhume.com',
'BAyb_WgaR0L0pODaR7wWkxJi__tWbM1MPBymyRDFEGjtDCWeRYS9EF7yGoCHLdHJi6hikYdg4MuY
    aK0XoD0qnoY',
  'p6YVD7t8HkABoez1CvVJ5bl7BnEdKUu5bSyVjyxMBh0'
);
                                                  Listen to POST
app.post('/register', function (req, res) {       requests at '/register'.

  var endpoint = req.body.endpoint;               Save the user's
                                                  registration details so
saveRegistrationDetails(endpoint, key, authSecret);   you can send messages
                                                  to them at a later stage.
  const pushSubscription = {
    endpoint: req.body.endpoint,
```

Build the push-Subscription object.

```
    keys: {
      auth: req.body.authSecret,
      p256dh: req.body.key
    }
  };

  var body = 'Thank you for registering';
  var iconUrl = 'https://example.com/images/homescreen.png';

  webpush.sendNotification(pushSubscription,          ◁─┐  Send the web
    JSON.stringify({                                     │  push message.
      msg: body,
      url: 'http://localhost:3111/',
      icon: iconUrl
    }))
    .then(result => res.sendStatus(201))
    .catch(err => { console.log(err); });
});

app.listen(3111, function () {
  console.log('Web push app listening on port 3111!')
});
```

Listing 6.2 starts by requiring the necessary Node.js modules. I've included the Web Push library as well as Node Express.

Before you can start sending messages, you need to set the VAPID settings. Remember that the VAPID key is needed to define a handshake between your app server and the push service and allows the push service to confirm which site is sending messages. Think of it as a simple identification card.

Next, you've created an endpoint that will listen to POST messages sent to '/register'. In this endpoint, you can read the subscription details sent through and save them in a database. You'll need to store the user's details in a database so that when you have something to push to them, you can cycle through their details and send it from the server. In this code sample, I haven't included how to save the user's subscription details; you can do that using your preferred database.

You're now ready to start sending push messages. Using the unique subscription details sent from the browser, the code in listing 6.2 then builds a pushSubscription object based on them. Finally, you fire off a push notification using the webpush.sendNotification() function with the user's unique details. In this push message, you thank them for registering.

To get the code in listing 6.2 fully working, you'll need to include a manifest.json file in your HTML page. The code in listing 6.2 also assumes you have a basic working understanding of Node.js. To learn about the code used in this example and see an end-to-end working solution, check out the GitHub repo for this chapter at bit.ly/chapter-pwa-6.

6.4.3   *Receiving and interacting with notifications*

Now that you've stored the user's unique subscription details, you can start sending push messages to them and provide them with timely updates on important notifications.

On the front-end code, you need to add some code to your Service Worker. The code in the next listing shows how to listen for the push event and display a push notification accordingly.

Listing 6.3   Receiving a push notification inside a Service Worker

```
self.addEventListener('push', function (event) {

  var payload = event.data ? JSON.parse(event.data.text()) : 'no payload';        ◁──

  var title = 'Progressive Times';
                                                                          Check to see if any
  event.waitUntil(                                                        payload data was
    self.registration.showNotification(title, {        ◁──               sent from the server.
      body: payload.msg,
      url: payload.url,
      icon: payload.icon                        Show a web push
    })                                          notification using the
  );                                            information provided.
});
```

The code in listing 6.3 listens to the push event and reads the payload of the data sent from the server. With this payload data, you can then display a notification using the showNotification function.

Hooray! You've sent your first web push notification. You should now notice this appear in the browser. But there's one more step. For the user to interact with the push notification, you need to handle the click event of the notification using the code in the following listing.

Listing 6.4   Handling user interaction with the push notification

```
self.addEventListener('notificationclick', function (event) {

  event.notification.close();                         ◁──   Close the notification tile
                                                            once you've clicked on it.
  event.waitUntil(                         ◁──
    clients.matchAll({
      type: "window"                    Check to see if the current
    })                                  window is already open
      .then(function (clientList) {     and focuses if it is.
        for (var i = 0; i < clientList.length; i++) {
          var client = clientList[i];
          if (client.url == '/' && 'focus' in client)
            return client.focus();
        }                                                      Open the
        if (clients.openWindow) {                              URL once
          return clients.openWindow('http://localhost:3111');  ◁──  clicked.
        }
      })
```

```
    );
});
```

The code in listing 6.4 will listen for the click event of the notification tile. Once it's been fired, it will close the notification tile and then open the window with the given URL. With all these pieces in place, the browser should now receive a push notification that looks like figure 6.5.

Figure 6.5 The code in the Service Worker listens for any push events and displays a notification with the data provided.

Once you've completed the necessary steps required to send a push notification, adding more notifications based on different events is much easier. The best part about the code you've seen in this chapter is that your users are able to start to engaging more deeply with experiences on the web even when they've closed the tab or navigated away.

Being able to send these messages is a great step forward for the web, but a basic push notification only allows the user to tap the message or dismiss it entirely. In order to take push notifications to the next level, you can use notification *actions* to truly engage with your users. Using notifications actions, you can define contextual actions that the user can invoke and interact with. These actions act as buttons and give the user a choice based on the next action they'd like to perform. Let's see how to add this functionality to your existing Progressive Times web app.

Some users receiving this notification will be on devices that have vibration functionality, such as mobile phones. To enable this vibration functionality, you can add a vibration pattern to the notification. A *vibration pattern* can either be an array of numbers or a single number that's treated as an array of one number. The values in the array represent times in milliseconds, with the even indices being how long to vibrate and the odd indices being how long to pause before the next vibration. Let's take this even further and see how to add vibration functionality to the push notification.

Listing 6.5 Adding notification actions and custom vibration patterns

```
self.addEventListener('push', function (event) {

  var payload = event.data ? JSON.parse(event.data.text()) : 'no payload';

  var title = 'Progressive Times';

  event.waitUntil(
    self.registration.showNotification(title, {
      body: payload.msg,
```

```
      url: payload.url,
      icon: payload.icon,
      actions: [                                          The actions to appear
        { action: 'voteup', title: 'Vote Up' },          on the notification
        { action: 'votedown', title: 'Vote Down' }],
      vibrate: [300, 100, 400]                            Vibrate for 300 ms, pause
    })                                                    for 100 ms, then vibrate
  );                                                      again for 400ms.
});
```

The code in listing 6.5 listens for any push events that are sent from the server and then shows a notification based on the payload information. When the showNotification function is invoked, you're adding an array of actions to the notification. These actions will appear on the notification and will look similar to figure 6.6.

Figure 6.6 Push notifications can be enhanced by using notification actions.

Next, you need to handle the click events for this notification, and the following listing shows how.

Listing 6.6 Handling notiification actions from within the Service Worker

```
self.addEventListener('notificationclick', function(event) {
                                                          Close the notification
  event.notification.close();                             tile once the user has
                                                          clicked on it.
  if (event.action === 'voteup') {
    clients.openWindow('http://localhost:/voteup');       Determine which action
  }                                                        was chosen by the user.
  else {
    clients.openWindow('http://localhost:/votedown');     Depending on their
  }                                                        choice, direct them
}, false);                                                 to the correct URL.
```

The code in listing 6.6 listens for the click event of the notification. Once it's fired, you can see the action that the user chose and direct them accordingly. The event .action property contains the user's choice, and you open a new browser window based on this.

When you put all these pieces together and the message is sent, it should look like figure 6.6. Push notifications allow your users to opt in to timely updates from sites they love and let you re-engage them with customized, engaging content.

Now that you have the basic tools required to start sending push notifications, your options are endless.

6.4.4 Unsubscribing

Users can unsubscribe themselves by changing a few settings in their browser, but there may come a time when you want to programmatically unsubscribe a user. For example, you could add a simple button to your web page that would allow users to unsubscribe at the tap of a button instead of digging around in their browser settings. The code in the following listing shows this in action.

Listing 6.7 Unsubscribing a user from push notifications

```html
<!DOCTYPE html>
<html>
  <head>
    <meta charset="UTF-8">
    <title>Progressive Times</title>
        <link rel="manifest" href="/manifest.json">

    <button type="button" id="unsubscribe">Unsubscribe</button>    ⟵  The
  </head>                                                               unsubscribe
  <body>                                                                button
  <script>
  function unsubscribe() {
if ('serviceWorker' in navigator) {
  navigator.serviceWorker.ready
    .then((serviceWorkerRegistration) => {                         Check to see
      serviceWorkerRegistration.pushManager.getSubscription()  ⟵  if the user
        .then((subscription) => {                                  has an
          if (!subscription) {                                     existing
            console.log("Not subscribed, nothing to do.");         subscription.
            return;
          }                                             If they're subscribed,
          subscription.unsubscribe()             ⟵     unsubscribe them.
            then(function() {
              console.log("Successfully unsubscribed!.");
            })
            .catch((e) => {
              logger.error('Error thrown while unsubscribing from push
    messaging', e);
            });
        });
    });
  }
}
```

```
document.getElementById("unsubscribe").addEventListener("click",
    unsubscribe);
```

Add an event listener
to the click event of the
unsubscribe button.

```
    </script>
    </body>
</html>
```

The code in listing 6.7 is a basic example that shows how you can unsubscribe a user
using a button. The listing contains code that will first check to see if the user is already
subscribed using the pushManager.getSubscription() function. If the user is subscribed,
you then unsubscribe them using the subscription.unsubscribe() function. Finally you
add an event listener to the button that will fire your unsubscribe code.

6.5 *Third-party push notifications*

As you can imagine, the business of sending push notifications to the many different
browsers out there can be tricky. If you'd prefer not to build your own push notification server and instead use a SaaS product, there are many third-party solutions out
there, such as the one shown in figure 6.7.

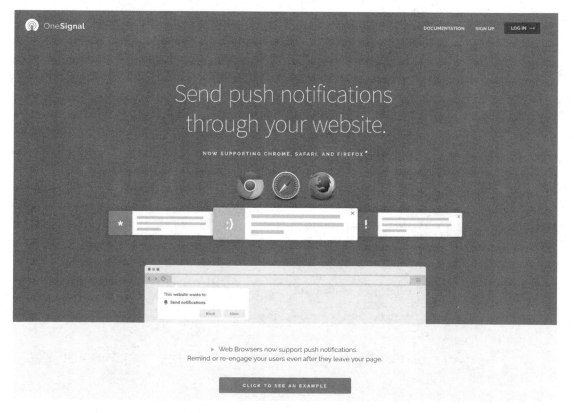

**Figure 6.7   Third-party services provide enhanced functionality and are a great way to send push notifications to
many users regardless of their browser support.**

Services such as OneSignal, Roost, and Aimtell all offer a solution that can target multiple browsers and provide you with enhanced functionality. Many of these services have created libraries to deal with all the major browsers, which means you'll get full coverage and engagement regardless of browser. These services also have a lot of functionality built into them that allows you to schedule messages for a later date, and some have complex reporting charts that give insight into how your users are interacting with your notifications.

6.6   *Summary*

Push notifications are a great way to engage with your users even after they navigate away from your site and close their browser window

In order to send push messages to a user, they first need to opt in. This provides the developer with unique subscription details based on the user's device and browser.

Once the user has opted in, it is important to save their subscription details in order to send messages to them.

VAPID is a specification that defines a handshake between your app server and the push service and allows the push service to confirm which site is sending messages.

Push notifications can be enhanced by using notification actions and even device vibration.

If you'd like to reach a wide range of browsers, some third-party services can deal with this.

Part 4

Resilient web applications

When I'm trying to access information on the go on my mobile phone, nothing is more frustrating than not being able to get to that information I need so desperately, especially when I know that I've viewed a certain web page before. Fortunately, you can build Progressive Web Apps (PWAs) to deal with such situations. In this part of the book, you'll learn how to build web apps that can work offline and deal with situations where you may be in an area with poor or no network coverage at all.

In chapter 7, you'll learn how to use the power of Service Workers to build resilient web apps that work with no connection. This chapter also covers some of the gotchas you should look out for when building an offline web app. By the end of the chapter, we will have a fully working example of an offline PWA using the sample application Progressive Times.

Chapter 8 shows you how to build PWAs that cater to situations where the user has a network connection, but it's slow, flaky, or prone to drop occasionally. Dealing with temperamental network connections can be tricky, but in this chapter, you'll learn the best techniques to build resilient web apps that work with poor or unreliable network connections.

In chapter 9, we'll take the offline web a step further and look at a new web API called BackgroundSync. Most offline websites may be read only, but you may want your users to continue working offline and sending information to the server. The BackgroundSync API allows users to queue data that needs to be sent to the server while the user is working offline—then as soon as they're online again, it sends the queued data to the server. We'll also dive into a soon-to-be-released feature called PeriodicSync that allows developers to schedule a sync for a predetermined time.

By the end of part 4, you'll have a clear understanding of how to build truly resilient web apps that work completely offline.

Offline browsing

7

During my daily commute to work, I travel via train into central London. Even though most of London has great cellular coverage, there arc times during my journey where the signal drops off or is so weak that I can't connect to the web. As a user, this experience can be extremely frustrating. In this chapter, you'll learn how to use the power of Service Workers to overcome this issue and build resilient web apps that work with no connection. This chapter also covers some of the gotchas you should look out for when building an offline web app. By the end of the chapter, you'll have a fully working example of an offline PWA using the sample application, Progressive Times. We'll also dive into how you can start tracking the ways your users are using your web app while offline using a clever offline tracking library.

7.1 *Unlocking the cache*

In chapter 3 you learned about using Service Worker caching to improve the performance and load times of your web pages. Using the sample application in this book, Progressive Times, you cached many of the resources required to achieve a lightning fast load times.

In this chapter, we're going to build on the example in chapter 3 and see how to serve offline web pages from the cache. In fact, you've already done most of the hard work—you need to update your Service Worker to determine whether a user is offline. To see how this might work, look at figure 7.1.

Using figure 7.1, imagine the following scenario: a user is browsing the Progressive Times web app. Stuck in their car without any network signal, they still try to load the web app. Under normal circumstances, this scenario would fail and present

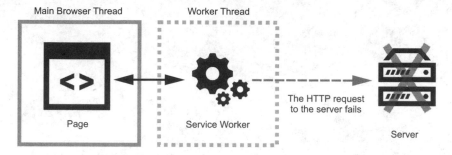

Figure 7.1   Using a Service Worker, you can determine whether the user is attempting to fetch a resource while they're offline.

the user with an "offline" screen. But because Service Workers are able to intercept HTTP requests, you can reliably determine whether anything went wrong while they were trying to request a resource.

In your Service Worker, you can check for any failed requests and decide to return a cached version of the page that the user is trying to view. In fact, you're in total control and could return anything that exists in cache. Using this simple technique, you can build web applications that work completely offline.

Let's step through the different stages involved in building an offline web application.

7.2   *Serving files while offline*

Before you begin updating your Progressive Times application, let's take a look at a basic offline example. First, imagine you've created a simple HTML page that displays a message letting the user know they're offline. Using your Service Worker, you'll return this "offline" page when a user has no connection.

The following listing breaks it down into smaller chunks in your Service Worker.

Listing 7.1   Adding an offline page into the Service Worker cache

```
'use strict';

const cacheName = 'offline-cache';          ⟵  Name of the
const offlineUrl = 'offline-page.html';          offline cache

                                            ⟵  URL for the offline
this.addEventListener('install', event => {      web page you'll store
  event.waitUntil(                               in the offline cache
    caches.open(cacheName).then(function(cache) {
      return cache.addAll([
          offlineUrl                        ⟵  Add offline web page into
      ]);                                       the cache during Service
    })                                          Worker installation
  );
});
```

Listing 7.1 adds an offline page that I've called offline-page.html into the cache during the installation of the Service Worker. With chapter 3 fresh in your mind, the code in listing 7.2 may look familiar—it's similar to the caching examples we looked at in chapter 3.

Now that the offline page is stored in cache, you can retrieve it whenever you need to, even if the user is offline. In the same Service Worker, the following listing adds the logic to return the offline page if we have no connectivity.

Listing 7.2 Serving an offline page when the user has no connectivity

Is user trying to navigate to another page? Check for a GET request and then see if they're requesting a resource of type 'text/html'.

If the fetch fails for any reason, catch this error.

```
this.addEventListener('fetch', event => {
  if (event.request.method === 'GET' &&
    event.request.headers.get('accept').includes('text/html')) {
    event.respondWith(
      fetch(event.request.url).catch(error => {
        return caches.match(offlineUrl);
      })
    );
  }
  else{
    event.respondWith(fetch(event.request));
  }
});
```

Return the offline page you cached during Service Worker installation.

Otherwise, respond as normal.

First, you're tapping into the fetch event and inspecting the HTTP headers to determine if the user is trying to make an HTTP GET request for an HTML web page. You're doing this because you only want this logic to take place if a user is trying to navigate to another web page (see the third line in listing 7.2). If they are, you add a catch() onto your JavaScript promise. With JavaScript promises, if any error occurs in the promise chain, the error is then bubbled up, and you can use catch() to determine what went wrong along the chain. In this case, you're using this catch() to determine if the HTTP request for the web page failed and the user has no connection. You then handle this error and return an "offline" page that you cached during service worker installation.

If a user is trying to open the Progressive Times app without a network connection, you want to ensure that you only show them an offline version when they're trying to navigate to another page. That way, if the user is trying to make a request for, say, a JavaScript file, the code will ignore it and continue as normal.

To test this in action, you can use a few techniques. You could unplug your network cable, disable your Wi-Fi, or use the Developer Tools built into your browser. (For quick feedback, the latter is my preferred solution.)

Firefox, Chrome, and Opera can all simulate offline mode from within the browser. In Firefox, choose File > Work Offline. Google Chrome and Opera have a handy tool built into their Developer Tools to help you test offline functionality. Start by opening the Developer Tools (found by browsing the menu) and heading to the Network tab. From there you can check the Offline check box.

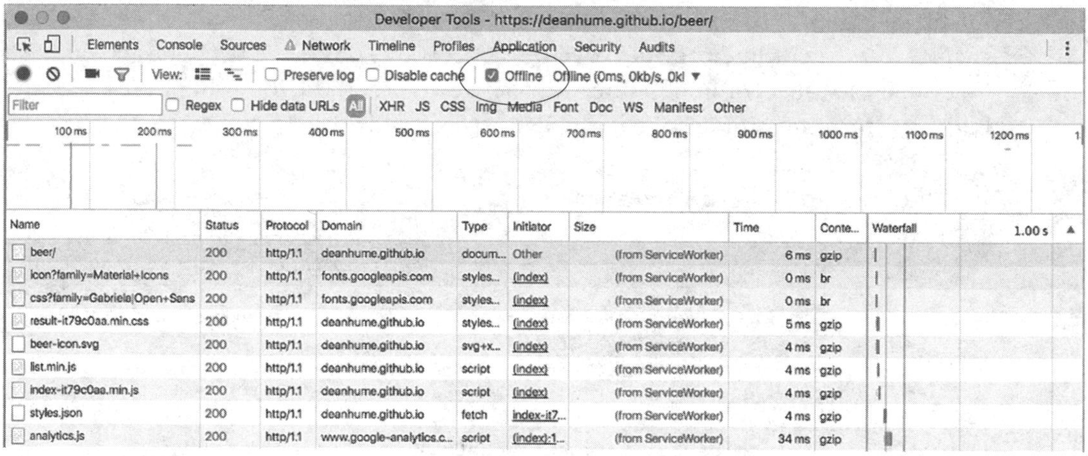

Figure 7.2 **Using the Developer Tools in Opera and Chrome, you can simulate an offline connection.**

Any requests made from this point onward will be offline, even if you're connected to the web. This simple technique is a great way to quickly test your offline logic. Just don't forget to uncheck the check box when you're done—failing to do so has left me scratching my head trying to figure out why I was offline many times before.

The code examples in listings 7.1 and 7.2 are useful but only return a single offline web page. Remember that in our sample application, Progressive Times, you pre-cached most of the pages during Service Worker installation. Let's see how to combine this technique with you code in the Progressive Times application.

To refresh your memory, let's take another look at the code you used chapter 3. The next listing adds code that will fall back to a default "offline" page if the user doesn't have the resource stored in their cache

Listing 7.3   Fall back to default offline page if a resource isn't already stored in cache

```
const cacheName = 'latestNews-v1';
const offlineUrl = 'offline-page.html';          ◁── URL of the
                                                      offline web page
self.addEventListener('install', event => {
  event.waitUntil(
    caches.open(cacheName)
    .then(cache => cache.addAll([
      './js/main.js',
      './js/article.js',
      './images/newspaper.svg',
      './css/site.css',
      './data/latest.json',
      './data/data-1.json',
```

```
      './article.html',
      './index.html',
      offlineUrl                    ←┐ Add in the offline page during
    ]))                              ┘ Service Worker install.
  );
});
                                           ┐ Event listener for
self.addEventListener('fetch', event => {  ┘ the fetch event
                                        ←

  event.respondWith(caches.match(event.request).then(function (response) {
    if (response) {
      return response;
    }
    var fetchRequest = event.request.clone();

    return fetch(fetchRequest).then(function (response) {
      if (!response || response.status !== 200) {
        return response;
      }

      var responseToCache = response.clone();
      caches.open(cacheName).then(function (cache) {
        cache.put(event.request, responseToCache);      ┐ If fetch event failed for any
      });                                                │ reason, check if it was for
                                                         │ an HTML page and if user
      return response;                                   │ was trying to navigate to
    }).catch(error => {                             ←┘   another page.
      if (event.request.method === 'GET' &&
      event.request.headers.get('accept').includes('text/html')) {
        return caches.match(offlineUrl);    ←┐
      }                                        Return offline page you stored
    });                                        in cache during the Service
  }));                                         Worker install step
});
```

The code in listing 7.3 uses a cache-first pattern described in chapter 3. The code starts off by adding an array of resources into cache during the Service Worker install step. You may notice a slight difference with this code: you're also adding your fallback offline web page into cache during the Service Worker install. You're doing this so that it's available in cache when you need it later.

Next, the code taps into the fetch event by adding an event listener. The first thing you want to do is check and see if the requested resource already exists in cache. If it does, you can return it at this point and go no further. But if the requested resource doesn't already exist in the cache, you make the request as originally intended and add the response into cache for a later stage. I've added a catch() onto the JavaScript promise that will get fired if the user tries to fetch the resource and it fails.

Inside catch() you check to see if the user was trying to navigate to another page with a GET request to fetch a resource of type text/html. If so, return the web page you already have stored in cache.

The code in listing 7.3 will always look in cache first and then fall back to the network if it doesn't find a resource in cache. If it can't retrieve the next web page over the network, it will fall back to a cached offline web page. The Progressive Times web app is now super-fast and also works offline.

As web developers, having this functionality at our fingertips is extremely powerful. Using a bit of creativity, you can build powerful offline web applications. For example, *The Guardian* newspaper in the U.K. displays an offline page with a crossword puzzle built into it.

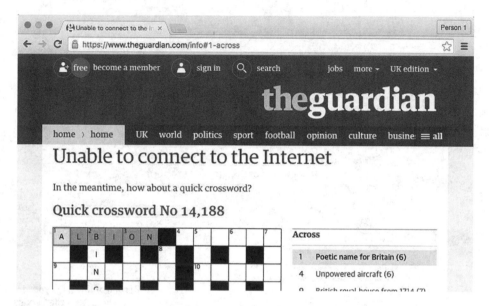

Figure 7.3   *The Guardian* website lets users play a crossword puzzle while they're offline.

Using *The Guardian* website, offline users can test their wits with a crossword puzzle. As soon as the user has a connection again, they can resume browsing the website.

Developers are only starting to unlock the power of the offline web. I'm excited to see how this progresses over the next few years.

7.3   A few gotchas to look out for

Being able to build an offline experience is a great step forward for the web. But as the saying goes, with great power comes great responsibility, and that goes for caching and the offline web experience.

As you read through this chapter, you may have wondered why you wouldn't cache the entire website during Service Worker installation. I know that when I found out I could serve offline pages, this question crossed my mind. But there's a fine line between offering a great experience for the user and asking them to download tons of content for pages that they may never visit. You don't want to land your users with a hefty mobile phone bill if they only visit one page of your web app.

Progressive Web Apps (PWAs) give us great power but can also be abused. If you find that your entire site could be cached in less than 500 KB, then perhaps it makes sense to cache everything, but if your entire site is 10 MB, it probably doesn't.

I like the way Jake Archibald's Offline Wikipedia (https://wiki-offline.jakearchibald .com) example works. It's a simple example of how a content site such as Wikipedia could offer offline content (see figure 7.4).

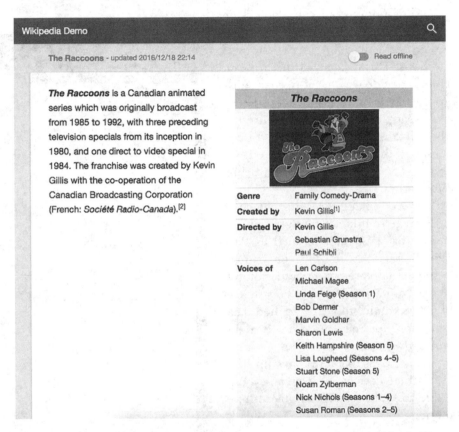

Figure 7.4   The Offline Wikipedia demo provides users with an option to download offline by toggling a flag.

When it comes to offline functionality, consider the needs and demographics of your users. How are your users accessing your site? Do they need the entire site down-loaded at once or can they fetch each new page as they visit? Answering these questions will help you determine your caching strategy. Only you can provide the answers to your users' needs.

7.4   *Cache isn't forever*

When I give talks about Service Workers and the Cache API, the question that almost always comes up is one about cache storage and what impact it has on the user's device. The reality is that each site has an amount of free space that's shared between all the other web-based storages including LocalStorage, IndexedDB, and Filesystem on the device.

The amount of storage available isn't permanent and it can differ completely between devices and current storage conditions. This means that the browser is free to decide whether it needs to discard the cached information in order to make space if conditions require it. Although this doesn't happen often, remember that it *could* be cleared, so don't base your entire website on being offline forever.

If you're looking for a more permanent storage solution, you might want to consider using something such as Persistent Storage.[1] At the time of writing, it's still in its early stages and not yet released officially, but the Persistence API allows you to store your cached data on a more permanent basis. It does require the user to give their consent because it means that it will take up storage on their device, but it means you'll be able to build a more durable offline experience.

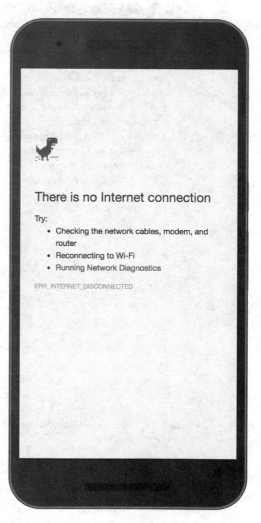

Figure 7.5   When a user has no internet connection, this is what they're used to seeing.

7.5   *Offline user experience*

As web developers, being able to build offline web experiences opens up a whole new world of possibilities for the user experience. Previously, users without a network connection would have been presented with a screen similar to figure 7.5.

---

[1]   https://developers.google.com/web/updates/2016/06/persistent-storage

The ability to display web pages without a network connection comes with a new set of user interface (UI) challenges. PWAs are a relatively new technology, and the average user may not even be aware that the web page they're viewing is available offline.

Many PWAs are already employing a few clever UI techniques to notify users that they're offline. Settled, an online company in the U.K. that helps people buy and sell homes, uses a technique in their PWA that displays a simple notification in the bottom of the screen, as shown in figure 7.6.

As soon as the user comes back online, the notification in figure 7.6 disappears, and the user becomes aware that they are online again.

I also like the way Flipkart greys out their PWA when the user is offline. Figure 7.7 shows both the online and offline versions of the Flipkart PWA.

Using inspiration from both the Flipkart and Settled PWAs, let's see how to add a basic notification to the sample application, Progressive Times, as shown in the following listing.

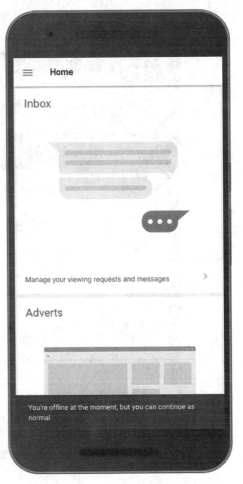

Figure 7.6 Settled's PWA notifies users that they're offline with a toast notification.

Listing 7.4 Showing a UI notification based on a user's connectivity

```
var offlineNotification = document.getElementById('offline');

function showIndicator() {
  offlineNotification.innerHTML = 'You are currently offline.';
  offlineNotification.className = 'showOfflineNotification';
}

function hideIndicator() {
  offlineNotification.className = 'hideOfflineNotification';
}

window.addEventListener('online',  hideIndicator);     #C
window.addEventListener('offline', showIndicator);     #D
```

This function is used to show an offline notification when the user is offline.

This function is used to hide the offline notification when the user is back online.

Online   Offline

Figure 7.7   Flipkart's PWA grays out the site to notify the user that they're offline.

In listing 7.5, you're adding an event listener to both the online and offline status of
the current browser window. If for any reason you lose connectivity, these events will
fire, and the appropriate function will be called. I've created two functions: one to
show an offline indicator when the user is offline, and one to hide the indicator when
the user comes back online. Using this simple technique, you can then give the user
feedback and let them know when they're offline.

This functionality that lets you determine whether a user is online or offline is built
into the browser by default. Believe it or not, browser support is also better than you
think; globally there is almost 95% support for this feature.[2] To learn more about this

---

[2] http://caniuse.com/#search=online

great browser feature, I recommend reading the Mozilla MDN documentation at http://bit.ly/navigator-online.

With this code now in place, a user will see something similar to figure 7.8 as soon as they lose network connectivity.

Figure 7.8 Basic UI feedback can be a useful way of letting your users know that they're offline.

The example in figure 7.8 is one of many types of options you can use to notify your users that they're offline.

All the code in this chapter is available on the GitHub repo for this book at bit.ly/chapter-pwa-7.

Being able to provide your users with this feedback is important and helps them trust that the web app will function when needed. In chapter 9, we'll look closely at Background Sync, a new web API that lets you defer actions until the user has stable connectivity. When combined with offline functionality, it can help you build offline web applications that ensure that whatever the user wants to send is sent.

7.6 Tracking offline usage

As the saying goes, if you can't measure it, you can't improve it. This is particularly relevant for offline web experiences. Remember that if your users are offline, you can't track them with your traditional web analytics approach. The analytics requests won't be able to fire without a connection, and the actions your users take will be lost.

Fortunately, an open source project called Service Worker Helpers[3] has you covered. It's a collection of Service Worker helper libraries to help you build your PWAs quickly and easily. One of these libraries is called Offline Google Analytics, and if you're currently using Google Analytics as your web analytics package, this is the library for you. Using a bit of clever Service Worker magic, the library will queue up any analytics requests while the user is offline, and as soon as they regain a connection, it sends the queued requests through to the analytics server.

To start using the library, you include it in your Service Worker file using the code in the following listing.

Listing 7.5   Tracking Google Analytics requests while offline

Import the library into the
service worker global scope

```
importScripts('../build/offline-google-analytics-import.js');    ⟵

goog.offlineGoogleAnalytics.initialize();                         ⟵

self.addEventListener('install', () => self.skipWaiting());       ⟵
self.addEventListener('activate', () => self.clients.claim());
```

Initialize the
Offline Google
Analytics
library

Have the Service Worker take
control as soon as possible

That's it! The library will now start queuing Google Analytics requests and only send them when it regains connection again. Using this library is a great way to ensure that you can track how your users use your web app while offline.

7.7   Summary

Using Service Workers, you can determine whether a user is offline while requesting a resource. At that point, you can decide whether you want to serve them something from the cache.

When building an offline web application, consider your caching strategy. A cache-first approach is great if your content doesn't change often, but you might consider a network-first approach for regularly changing content.

It's important to think about your users when building an offline experience. Downloading too much data may end up costing them, especially if they don't visit your entire site.

Service Worker cache isn't forever. If you're looking for something more long term, you might want to consider using Persistent Storage.

Consider your user experience (UX) approach when building an offline experience. Keep your users notified when they're offline and when they're back online.

Using the Service Worker Helpers library, you can track your offline usage with Google Analytics.

---

[3] https://github.com/GoogleChrome/sw-helpers

Building more resilient applications

As you've progressed through this book, you've learned how to build Progressive Web Apps (PWAs) that are lightning-fast and offer the user an engaging and interactive experience. In chapter 7, you found out how to build a PWA that caters to situations in which the user may not have a network connection. There may also be situations in which the user has a network connection but it's really slow or flaky or may drop occasionally. In this chapter, you'll learn about the best techniques to build resilient web apps that work with poor or unreliable network connections. By the end of this chapter, you'll have a clear understanding of how to build *truly* resilient web apps.

8.1 Network issues that modern websites face

Whether the user is in a building in New York with high-speed Wi-Fi or on safari in South Africa with a flaky 2G connection, all modern websites face the same connectivity issues. One of my favorite observations about the challenges of network connections comes from a book by Ilya Grigorik, entitled *High Performance Browser Networking* (O'Reilly, 2013):

> *Users dislike slow applications, but broken applications, due to transient network errors, are the worst experience of all. Your mobile application must be robust in the face of common networking failures: unreachable hosts, sudden drops in throughput or increases in latency, or outright loss of connectivity.*

He goes on to say the following:

> *Unlike the tethered world, you simply cannot assume that once the connection is established, it will remain established. The user may be on the move and may enter an area with high amounts of interference, many active users, or plain poor coverage.*

111

I think these two statements perfectly explain the situation that modern web developers face. Even if you build an extremely beautiful and fast website, it will still have to fetch resources over a network that can be prone to failure. That's why it's so important to build sites that are fast, engaging, and most of all *reliable*.

In the next section, we'll take a close look at two network challenges that web developers face: *lie-fi* and single *point of failure*.

8.1.1   *Understanding lie-fi and single point of failure*

On my commute, as I've mentioned, there are many spots along the journey that have a flaky connection. Sometimes my phone will engage in *lie-fi*—telling me there's a full strength signal, yet I can't download anything.

Lie-fi can result in a poor experience because the browser will persist in trying to download resources instead of giving up when it should and using a fallback. For most websites, lie-fi can be worse than being offline because if your site is offline, you can at least take appropriate action. We're going to look at a technique to help you deal with lie-fi and respond appropriately when the user encounters poor connectivity.

Quite often, you may add third-party scripts such as jQuery, social sharing buttons, or tracking scripts to your website with the best of intentions, but depending on the way these scripts are loaded, you could potentially create a front-end single point of failure (SPOF) that can block the site. According to Wikipedia (https://en.wikipedia.org/wiki/Single_point_of_failure), a SPOF is "a part of a system that, if it fails, will stop the entire system from working." If these third-party scripts aren't implemented and deployed properly, they pose a significant risk for the websites that host them.

Think about our Progressive Times newspaper application. Before the browser can render a page parsing the HTML markup, the web app loads web fonts using Google Fonts to improve its look and feel. During this process, whenever the parser encounters a script or CSS file, it has to stop and execute it before it can continue parsing the HTML. This is default behavior for the browser and it means that both CSS and JavaScript files will block the page loading until they've finished downloading.

If for any reason a third-party site referenced in the web page takes too long to load or is down, the Progressive Times app will be affected, as shown in figure 8.1. Unfortunately, this is completely outside of your control—the third-party servers are maintained separately from your own and you have to hope that they will function as expected. Well, fear not. We'll shortly look at how you can use Service Workers to ensure that your PWA can deal with such issues.

Figure 8.1 shows a fully loaded web page that isn't affected by SPOF—the site loads in around 1.1 seconds. On the right is a blank white screen that has been affected by a third-party SPOF and still hasn't finished loading after almost 17 seconds. The user is completely blocked and unable to interact with the site.

If you ever want to test what this might look like on your own website, try webpagetest.org (figure 8.2). It's free and among its many uses can be used to test SPOF. To do so, head to WebPagetest.org, enter the URL of the page you'd like to test, and

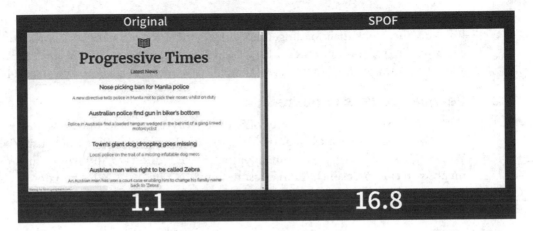

Figure 8.1   On the left, a fully working website, and on the right a website experiencing SPOF. If a third-party server is down or experiencing issues, your site will be affected too.

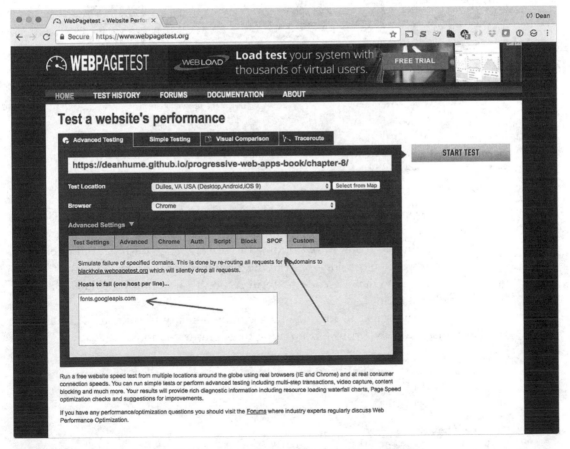

Figure 8.2   If a third-party server is down or running slowly, your site may be affected.

choose the SPOF tab. Behind the scenes, the site will search for these third-party libraries and block their loading, allowing you to test under network conditions.

From there, you can enter a list of third-party domains that will be "blocked" by WebPagetest.org, allowing you to simulate how it might affect your site in real life.

8.2 Service Workers to the rescue

Fortunately, you can use the power of Service Workers to build web apps that have fallbacks when issues such as lie-fi or SPOF occur. Remember that when using Service Workers, you're in complete control of the HTTP requests to and from your site. This means you can force an HTTP request to time out if it takes too long to download or if the user loses connectivity. Figure 8.3 shows this in action in our Progressive Times application.

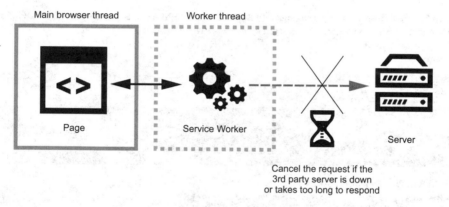

Figure 8.3 Using Service Workers, you can cancel the HTTP request if the third-party server takes too long to respond.

Using the diagram in figure 8.3, let's relate this to the Progressive Times app. In the web app, you're loading external web fonts from Google servers. If for any reason this HTTP request took too long to respond or the servers were down, it could delay the loading of your web app considerably, causing a SPOF. Let's see how to update the Progressive Times app to include code that will respond with an appropriate fallback if you experience a failure.

The code in the next listing may look familiar—it's quite similar to the Service Worker registration code you've been using throughout the book.

Listing 8.1 Basic web page that registers a Service Worker

```
<!DOCTYPE html>
<html>
 <head>
  <meta charset="UTF-8">
  <title>Progressive Times - Online News</title>
 </head>
```

```
<body>
    <script>
            if ('serviceWorker' in navigator) {
            navigator.serviceWorker.register('./service-
    worker.js').then(function(registration) {
            }).catch(function(err) {
                    console.log('ServiceWorker registration failed: ', err);
                });
            }
    </script>
</body>
</html>
```

Register the Service Worker.

Registration has failed.

Now that you've registered your Service Worker, you need to update it slightly to ensure that you can cater to scenarios such as lie-fi or SPOF. Ideally, you need to force the request to time out if it takes too long to respond.

The code in listing 8.2 contains the contents of the Service Worker file that you registered in listing 8.1. It contains a clever technique that I learned from Patrick Haman, a developer at Fastly. I recommend checking out his talk "Embracing the Network" (https://vimeo.com/163933605) to learn more about building systems that embrace the unpredictability of networks and defend against it all costs.

> **Listing 8.2   Service Worker code that returns a 408 response on slow networks**

```
function timeout(delay) {
    return new Promise(function (resolve, reject) => {
        setTimeout(function(){
            resolve(new Response('', {
                status: 408,
                statusText: 'Request timed out.'
            }));
        }, delay);
    });
};

self.addEventListener('fetch', function(event) {
if (/googleapis/.test(event.request.url)) {
    event.respondWith(Promise.race([timeout(3000),fetch(event.request.url)]));
} else {
    event.respondWith(fetch(event.request));
}
});
```

Classic timeout function that has been updated to return as a promise

Execute the timeout function using the passed in delay (amount in milliseconds).

If timeout occurs, return a new Response of status code 408 and provide a message.

Use a Promise.race condition to fire both the timeout and fetch function at the same time.

Otherwise make the request as expected.

Only run this check for requests to the domain googleapis.com .

Let's break that code down into smaller chunks. First, you're creating a function that executes a classic JavaScript timeout function, but with a slight twist. The function has been updated to return as a JavaScript promise. If for any reason this function does time out, it will return a new `Response` object. Remember that with Service Workers, you can build your own custom HTTP responses if required. Here you're constructing a custom HTTP response that will return a 408 HTTP status code with a custom message. You're going to use this HTTP response if your request takes too long to respond.

Next, you're using a `JavaScript Promise.race()` function. This function returns a promise that resolves or rejects as soon as one of the promises in the array resolves or rejects, with the value or reason from that promise (check out www.promisejs.org/patterns/#race). This idea behind this function is that you "race" a number of functions against each other and wait for the first one to return. Think of each function as a horse in a race—the fastest one (function) will win. This is perfect for this scenario, because if the `fetch` request wins, you return the resource as expected. But if the `timeout` function wins, you can assume that something took longer than expected, and you should return a fallback.

You may also notice that you've passed in a value of `3000` to the `timeout` function. This means 3000 milliseconds, or 3 seconds. You'll want to tweak this amount of time slightly to match the needs of your users. If you're looking for a guideline on that, note that according to a study by the Nielsen Norman Group (www.nngroup.com/articles/response-times-3-important-limits), "10 seconds is about the limit for keeping the user's attention." You should definitely set your limit to less than that.

That's it—you're now ready to test this in action. One of the best ways to simulate this functionality is to use the built-in throttling functionality in the browser. Google Chrome's Developer Tools can simulate a slower network connection. To get started, fire up your Developer Tools in Google Chrome and head over to the Network tab. From there, check Disable Cache and choose an option for throttling from the dropdown menu. I chose from the presets GPRS 50KB (figure 8.4). This is the slowest connection available and in most cases should force the code to return the fallback. If you refresh the web page and view the network requests, you'll be able to see the Service Worker take control of the requests.

Using this simulation technique, the `timeout` function will execute, and the Service Worker will return the custom HTTP response with a 408 status code, as shown in figure 8.5.

As you can see, the web fonts haven't loaded because the logic in the Service Worker took control and returned a custom HTTP response when the request took too long. This may not be ideal for the aesthetic look and feel of the site, but it means the user can continue as normal. Being able to interact with a site is a lot better than waiting for fonts to arrive.

Using Service Workers to reduce the unpredictability of network connectivity is a useful way to ensure that your site is available and isn't at the mercy of third-party servers. If you'd like to experiment with this code, check out the GitHub repository for this book at bit.ly/chapter-pwa-8.

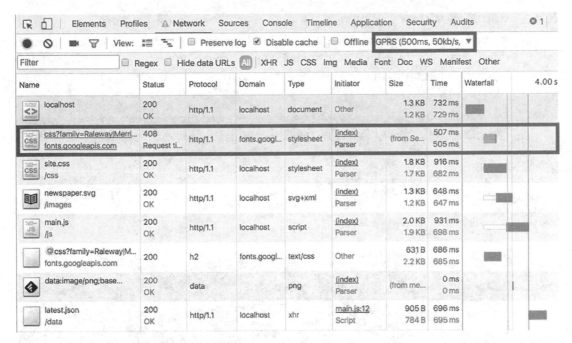

Name	Status	Protocol	Domain	Type	Initiator	Size	Time	Waterfall	4.00 s
localhost	200 OK	http/1.1	localhost	document	Other	1.3 KB 1.2 KB	732 ms 729 ms		
css?family=Raleway|Merri... fonts.googleapis.com	408 Request ti...	http/1.1	fonts.googl...	stylesheet	(index) Parser	(from Se...	507 ms 505 ms		
site.css /css	200 OK	http/1.1	localhost	stylesheet	(index) Parser	1.8 KB 1.7 KB	916 ms 682 ms		
newspaper.svg /images	200 OK	http/1.1	localhost	svg+xml	(index) Parser	1.3 KB 1.2 KB	648 ms 647 ms		
main.js /js	200 OK	http/1.1	localhost	script	(index) Parser	2.0 KB 1.9 KB	931 ms 698 ms		
css?family=Raleway|M... fonts.googleapis.com	200	h2	fonts.googl...	text/css	Other	631 B 2.2 KB	686 ms 685 ms		
data:image/png;base...	200 OK	data		png	(index) Parser	(from me...	0 ms 0 ms		
latest.json /data	200 OK	http/1.1	localhost	xhr	main.js:12 Script	905 B 784 B	696 ms 695 ms		

Figure 8.4 Using the built-in network throttling in Google Chrome, you can simulate a slow response and force a request to timeout (highlighted in red).

Figure 8.5 If the resource is blocked, the Service Worker will return a 408 HTTP response, meaning the fonts are missing from the page but the page still loads as expected.

8.3   *Using Workbox*

In the coding example in listing 8.2, you rolled your own code that handled lie-fi and third-party SPOF. Earlier in this book, I mentioned a helper library called Workbox, a handy set of libraries that will help you get started building powerful PWAs in no time (figure 8.6).

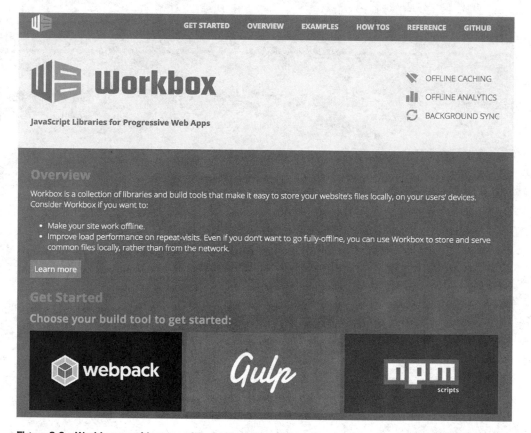

Figure 8.6   Workbox provides you with simple helpers for use in creating your own Service Workers.

The next listing looks at the same example we used in listing 8.2, but this time using Workbox to simplify the code a little.

Listing 8.3   Workbox with network timeout

```
importScripts('workbox-sw.prod.v1.1.0.js');

const workboxSW = new self.WorkboxSW();

workboxSW.router.registerRoute('https://fonts.googleapis.com/(.*)',
workboxSW.strategies.cacheFirst({
cacheName: 'googleapis',
```

Here choose to cache everything that matches the origin domain "googleapis.com".

Next, you're choosing to cache the resource using a cache-first strategy.

```
networkTimeoutSeconds: 4
})
);
```

◁──┐ **If the network request takes longer than four seconds to respond, fall back to the cached version.**

The code in listing 8.3 is a neat way to ensure that your resource will time out accordingly if the network request encounters a situation where lie-fi or SPOF might occur. Workbox uses an *express style* approach to routing, which means you can provide it with regex and paths that might match a request for a resource.

In the code in listing 8.3, you're using a cache-first approach and retrieving all assets that match the domain googleapis.com.

You may also notice that the `origin` property is using a regex approach to check any incoming requests. The code will check any incoming requests that match the origin `googleapis.com`. This code is similar to the code in listing 8.2.

As you can see, Workbox wraps up the code neatly and keeps your functionality concise. Another great thing about this library is that you get a lot of functionality for very little code.

8.4 Summary

It's important to build sites that are fast, engaging, and most of all *reliable*.

Web developers today all face the same network challenges: unreachable hosts, sudden drops in throughput or increases in latency, or outright loss of connectivity—all of which can provide a poor experience for the user.

Using Service Workers, you can build web apps that are resilient to flaky network conditions and fallback.

Lie-fi refers to when your browser behaves as if it has connectivity when, for whatever reason, it doesn't.

A single point of failure (SPOF) can occur when a third-party server goes down or isn't functioning as expected. This can unfortunately affect the performance of your own site and provide a poor experience for your users.

Using Service Workers, you can write code that will respond with an appropriate fallback if a site experiences a network failure.

You can use Workbox to neatly wrap up your code and provide you with network timeout functionality.

Webpagetest.org is a great resource for simulating SPOF as well as testing the overall performance of your website.

Keeping your data synchronized

Chapter 8 talked about building resilient Progressive Web Apps (PWAs) that can handle flaky or intermittent network connections. In this chapter, we'll take the offline web a step further and look at a new web API called BackgroundSync. This API allows users to queue data that needs to be sent to the server while a user is working offline, and then as soon as they're online again, it sends the queued data to the server. This is useful for when you want to ensure that what your user submits to the server truly gets sent. To give you a quick example of this on a practical level, say a user needs to be able to edit the details of a blog post using a Content Management System (CMS). If the CMS uses Service Workers and BackgroundSync, the user can edit the contents of the blog post offline, and then the CMS will sync the results when the user is online again. This functionality allows users to work on the go, regardless of whether they're connected to the internet.

By the end of the chapter, you'll know a lot about BackgroundSync and how you can start using it in your web apps today. We'll also dive into a soon-to-be-released feature called Periodic Sync that allows developers to schedule a sync for a predetermined time.

9.1 Understanding BackgroundSync

So far, we've been focusing on building websites that can function when the user is offline and dealing with situations where unreliable networks can cause failures. This functionality is great, but until now most of these pages have been *read-only*—you're only loading web pages and displaying information. What if you wanted the user to send something to the server while the user is offline? For example, they may want to save something important using their web app, safe in the knowledge that when they re-establish a network connection, their important information will be sent through to the server. BackgroundSync was built to handle that scenario.

BackgroundSync is a new web API that lets you defer actions until the user has stable connectivity, which makes it great for ensuring that whatever the user wants to send is sent when they regain connectivity. For example, let's say someone using the Progressive Times web app wants to contact the editors using the app offline. With BackgroundSync, they can "send" a contact message while offline, and once they regain connectivity, the Service Worker will send the message in the background. I like to think of this feature as the outbox of an email client: messages are queued up in the outbox, and as soon as there is a connection, they're sent.

This chapter runs through a simple example that shows you how to use BackgroundSync to ensure that your requests are queued even when the user is offline. We're going to take a look at the Progressive Times web app and see how to update it so that it can queue and sync offline requests.

9.1.1 Getting started

First you'll put the BackgroundSync API into action in our Progressive Times web app. I've created a new page called contact.html that allows a user to send a message to the editors. It contains a few input fields that will be used to send data to the server, as shown in the following listing.

Listing 9.1   An HTML contact page

```html
<!DOCTYPE html>
<html>
 <head>
  <meta charset="UTF-8">
  <title>Contact Page</title>
 </head>
<body>
  <div id="offline"></div>
  <!-- header -->
  <div id="header">
    <img id="logo" src="./images/newspaper.svg" />
    <h1>Progressive Times</h1>
    <br>
    <h6>Please send us any questions you may have!</h6>
  </div>
  <div id="container">
    <!-- contact form -->
    <div class="contact-form">
      <input type="text" id="name" name="name" placeholder="Your Name">
      <br>
      <input type="email" id="email" name="email" placeholder="Email Address">
      <br>
      <input type="text" id="subject" name="subject" placeholder="Subject">
      <br>
      <input type="text" id="message" name="message" placeholder="Your Message">
      <br>
```

The contact form fields

```
        <button id="submit">Send</button>
      </div>
    </div>
  </body>
</html>
```

The submit button that's used to send data to the server

The code in listing 9.1 contains the HTML markup for a simple page that the user will use to submit a message on the Progressive Times web app. The page isn't anything fancy, but serves as a good example of how BackgroundSync might work in the real world, as shown in figure 9.1. You'll update this page so it uses BackgroundSync and queues any requests when the user is offline.

Before you can go any further, you need to register the Service Worker in the HTML markup for this page. The code in the following listing that you're using to register the Service Worker may seem familiar, but this time you need to do things slightly differently when registering a sync. Don't worry if this doesn't all make sense—we'll be digging deeper, and I'll explain more shortly.

Figure 9.1   The contact form for the Progressive Times web application

---

Listing 9.2   Registering a BackgroundSync

Include the idb-keyval script in the page.

Once the Service Worker is ready, you can use the registration object.

```
<script src="./js/idb-keyval.js" ></script>
<script>
    if ('serviceWorker' in navigator && 'SyncManager' in window) {
      navigator.serviceWorker.register('./sw.js')
      .then(registration => navigator.serviceWorker.ready)
      .then(registration => {
        document.getElementById('submit').addEventListener('click', () => {
```

Check whether the current browser supports Service Workers.

Add an event listener to the click event of the submit.

```
        registration.sync.register('contact-email').then(() => {
  var payload = {
    name: document.getElementById('name').value,
    email: document.getElementById('email').value,
    subject: document.getElementById('subject').value,
    message: document.getElementById('message').value,
  };

  idbKeyval.set('sendMessage', payload);
        });
      });
    });
  }

</script>
```

Register a sync for this event and tag it with contact-email.

Get the payload of data from the page and save to an indexedDb.

That code may look a little scary. Let's break it down. At first glance, you may not have noticed that I included a library called idb-keyval, a lightweight, easy-to-use, promise-based store implemented with IndexedDB.[1] Chapter 1 discussed how Service Workers only have limited access to all the features of a browser—they have no access to the DOM and can't modify elements of a web page. But they *do* have access to IndexedDB and the cache storage. That's why you need to store the values of the POST request when the sync is initiated, so it can be accessed by the Service Worker when the sync event occurs. As we break down listing 9.2, why you need to choose this approach will make sense.

Understanding IndexedDB

IndexedDB is a low-level API for client-side storage of significant amounts of structured data, including files or blobs. This API uses indexes to enable high-performance searches of this data. Although DOM storage is useful for storing smaller amounts of data, it's less useful for storing larger amounts of structured data. This is where IndexedDB fits in—it's a better solution when it comes to large amounts of data.

Back to the code. First, you do a simple check to see if the browser supports Service Workers. If it does, register a file called sw.js. This file contains the Service Worker code with all the BackgroundSync magic. You're going to create this shortly.

Next, if the registration is successful and the Service Worker is ready, add a `click` event to the button and register a sync with the tag `contact-email`. This is a simple string that I've named to help me recognize this event. You can think of these sync tags as simple labels for different actions. You can have as many as you want. Here's the line:

```
registration.sync.register('contact-email')
```

---

[1] https://github.com/jakearchibald/idb-keyval

You're registering a sync using the registration object and providing it with a tag to identify it. Each sync must have a unique tag name because if you register a sync using the same tag as a pending sync, they will combine together. If the user tries to send seven messages while offline, they'll only get one sync when they regain connectivity. If you did want this to happen seven times, you need to use seven unique tag names.

Finally, you retrieve the values from the different input fields that the user entered on the page and save them into the IndexedDB. With these values stored safely in the IndexedDB, you can retrieve them when the sync event takes place in the Service Worker.

9.1.2   *The Service Worker*

Before BackgroundSync will function correctly, you need to update the Service Worker code. The following listing contains the code that will respond to your newly created sync event.

Listing 9.3   Responding to a sync event

Add an event listener for the sync event.

Check the tag of the current sync to ensure that you fire the correct code.

Get the payload values from the IndexedDB.

Use fetch API to POST to the server.

```
importScripts('./js/idb-keyval.js');
self.addEventListener('sync', (event) => {
  if (event.tag === 'contact-email') {
    event.waitUntil(
      idbKeyval.get('sendMessage').then(value =>
        fetch('/sendMessage/', {
          method: 'POST',
          headers: new Headers({ 'content-type': 'application/json' }),
          body: JSON.stringify(value)
        })));

        idbKeyval.delete('sendMessage');
  }
});
```

Pass in the payload values that you retrieved from the IndexedDB.

Remove the payload values from the IndexedDB.

Listing 9.3 adds an event listener for the sync event. This event will only fire when the browser believes that the user has connectivity.[2] You may also notice that I've added a check to confirm that the current event has a tag that matches the string 'contact-email'. This tag was added to the submit button (listing 9.2) when you registered the Service Worker for this page. If you didn't have this tag, the sync event would fire every time the user had connectivity and process your logic repeatedly.

Next, you retrieve the payload values that were stored in the IndexedDB when the user clicked the submit button. With these values, you then use the fetch API to POST the values to the server. The last step in the logic is to clean up afterwards and remove

---

[2] https://github.com/WICG/BackgroundSync/blob/master/explainer.md

the values that are stored in the IndexedDB to ensure that you don't have any old data lying around.

If all these steps were successful, the `fetch` request will return a successful result. If for any reason the `fetch` request wasn't successful, the BackgroundSync API will try again. BackgroundSync has some clever retry functionality built into it to deal with a situation where the promise might fail. Figure 9.2 illustrates the retry logic.

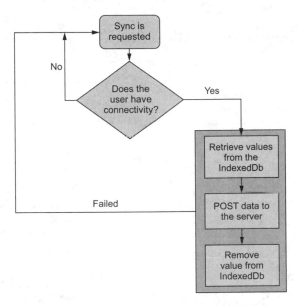

Figure 9.2   The retry logic for BackgroundSync

Like most Service Worker–based code, BackgroundSync expects a promise because it needs to signal to the browser that the `sync` event is ongoing, and it needs to keep the Service Worker active if possible. If for any reason the fetch request failed and it received a promise that rejected, it will signal the browser that the sync failed, and this will cause the browser to reschedule the event. This functionality is handy when you want to ensure that what your user submits gets sent.

Under the hood, the browser might combine syncs together to reduce the number of times that the current device, network connection (radio), and browser need to wake up. Although these event timings may be combined, you still get a new event per pending sync.

9.1.3   *Provide a fallback*

BackgroundSync is a relatively new API, which means older browsers don't support it. As with most of the Service Worker code you've been using throughout this book, providing a fallback for BackgroundSync is straightforward.

The next listing updates listing 9.2 slightly to provide a fallback for browsers that don't support BackgroundSync.

Listing 9.4   Fallback for browsers that don't support backgroundsync

Check to see whether current browser supports Service Workers and SyncManager.

```
<script src="/js/idb-keyval.js" ></script>
<script>
  if ('serviceWorker' in navigator && 'SyncManager' in window) {
    navigator.serviceWorker.register('./sw.js')
    .then(registration => navigator.serviceWorker.ready)

    .then(registration => {
      document.getElementById('submit').addEventListener('click', () => {

        registration.sync.register('contact-email').then(() => {

  var payload = {
    name: document.getElementById('name').value,
    email: document.getElementById('email').value,
    subject: document.getElementById('subject').value,
    message: document.getElementById('message').value,
  };

  idbKeyval.set('sendMessage', payload);

        });
      });
    });
  } else {
  document.getElementById('submit').addEventListener('click', () => {
  var payload = {
    name: document.getElementById('name').value,
    email: document.getElementById('email').value,
    subject: document.getElementById('subject').value,
    message: document.getElementById('message').value,
  };

  fetch('/sendMessage/',
  {
      method: 'POST',
      headers: new Headers({
        'content-type': 'application/json'
      }),
      body: JSON.stringify(payload)
  });
});
}

</script>
```

Add an event listener to the click event of the submit button.

Get the values from the input fields on the contact form.

Use the fetch API to post the values to the server.

The code in listing 9.4 adds some extra logic to provide a fallback for browsers that don't support the BackgroundSync API. First, the code is checking to see whether Service Workers are supported and tests to see whether the current browser supports the SyncManager feature. The SyncManager interface of the ServiceWorker API provides an interface for registering and listing sync registrations. If the browser does support SyncManager, you can continue and register the tag as expected. But if Service Workers aren't supported or the browser doesn't support the API, you continue and post the request to the server as expected. With this code in place, you cover all your bases, and it's a win-win solution for your users: they get the bonus of BackgroundSync if their browser supports it and normal functionality if it doesn't.

To test this chapter's code for yourself, download it from the GitHub repository at bit.ly/chapter-pwa-9. The code includes a server-side implementation used to simulate a POST event for the contact details discussed throughout this chapter. To get started with the PWA, you'll need to have Node.js installed (which you've used in previous chapters). If you're not familiar with Node.js, don't worry—these code listings serve as mere examples, which means you can use any server-side language you like. Once you have Node.js installed and the repository in place, you can fire up the PWA by running the following command in your terminal:

```
npm install && node server.js
```

When the application is up and running, head to http://localhost:3111/contact to start experimenting with this page.

9.1.4 Testing

Believe it or not, testing all this is easier than you think: once you've visited the page and your Service Worker is active, all you need to do is disconnect from the network by unplugging the network cable, disabling your Wi-Fi, or changing your network connection using the Developer Tools.

When I first started testing this feature, I disabled the Wi-Fi connection on my laptop, submitted the contact details, and then re-enabled the Wi-Fi connection (figure 9.3).

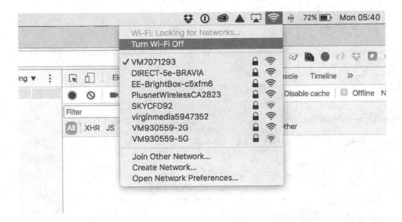

Figure 9.3   To test BackgroundSync, disable your network connection.

If I view the network requests while offline, no HTTP requests take place, but as soon as I re-enable the network connection, the queued request is sent to the server and is visible in the Network view of the Developer Tools, as shown in figure 9.4.

Figure 9.4   When you lose network connection your event will be synced and will be sent to the server when the user regains connectivity. The sync event is highlighted in red.

9.2   *Notifying the user*

As we've been discussing, the message will indeed be sent to the server when the user regains connectivity, but unfortunately the user won't know this has happened. Remember, a lot of users don't even know the web is capable of working offline, which is why it's important to provide feedback to users and let them know that the message has been queued and will be sent when they are online again.

In chapter 7, you built a simple notification that notifies the user when they're offline. Using a similar technique, you can let the user know that the message has been queued and will be sent. The next listing updates your Service Worker registration code slightly to include this UI notification.

Listing 9.5   Notifying the user that the message has been queued

```
<script src="/js/idb-keyval.js" ></script>

<script>
function displayMessageNotification (notificationText){
  var messageNotification = document.getElementById('message');
  messageNotification.innerHTML = notificationText;
  messageNotification.className = 'showMessageNotification';
}

  if ('serviceWorker' in navigator && 'SyncManager' in window) {

    navigator.serviceWorker.register('./sw.js')
    .then(registration => navigator.serviceWorker.ready)

    .then(registration => {
      document.getElementById('submit').addEventListener('click', () => {

        registration.sync.register('contact-email').then(() => {

  var payload = {
    name: document.getElementById('name').value,
    email: document.getElementById('email').value,
    subject: document.getElementById('subject').value,
    message: document.getElementById('message').value,
  };

  idbKeyval.set('sendMessage', payload);
displayMessageNotification('Message queued');

      });
    });
  });
```

Function to show the notification and notify user of message status

Show notification and let user know the message is queued to be sent

```
} else {
document.getElementById('submit').addEventListener('click', () => {
var payload = {
  name: document.getElementById('name').value,
  email: document.getElementById('email').value,
  subject: document.getElementById('subject').value,
  message: document.getElementById('message').value,
};
fetch('/sendMessage/',
{
    method: 'post',
    headers: new Headers({
      'content-type': 'application/json'
    }),
    body: JSON.stringify(payload)
})
.then(displayMessageNotification('Message sent'))
.catch((err) => displayMessageNotification('Message failed'));
}

</script>
```

⟵ **Try to send message using traditional method**

⟵ **Show notification and let user know the notification was sent**

You may notice listing 9.5 hasn't changed much from listing 9.3. You've added code to display a message notification once the sync has been registered or, in the case of older browsers, the message has been sent.

I find it helpful to visualize what the code in a listing might look like. To give you an idea, figure 9.5 shows what this notification might look like on a mobile device.

The notification isn't anything fancy—just a simple HTML element with feedback for the user. Using this simple technique is a great way to provide your users with feedback when they submit information to the server.

9.3   *Periodic synchronization*

Imagine the following scenario: a user opens up their phone to see that they already have the latest news for the Progressive Times App—which is strange because they're currently offline and haven't visited the web app today. Instead, a sync happened in the background while they were sleeping. New data was synced to their phone before they even woke up and was available for them in an instant. Very impressive!

Figure 9.5   Once the user has submitted the form, update the UI to let them know that it has been sent successfully regardless of whether they're online or offline.

This feature, known as PeriodicSync, allows you to schedule a sync for a predetermined time. It's simple to set up, doesn't require any server configuration, and allows the browser to optimize when it fires in order to be helpful and less disruptive to the user.

At the time of writing, PeriodicSync is still being developed (and is therefore subject to change), but it will be available in browsers shortly.[3] It is powerful functionality that's worth sharing, which is why I wanted to include it in the book at this early stage. The following listing gives you an idea of what this code might look like when it is released.

Listing 9.6   Registering a PeriodicSync

```
navigator.serviceWorker.ready.then(function(registration) {
  registration.periodicSync.register({
    tag: 'get-latest-news',
    minPeriod: 12 * 60 * 60 * 1000,
    powerState: 'avoid-draining'
    networkState: 'avoid-cellular'
  }).then(function(periodicSyncReg) {

    // success
  }, function() {
    // failure
  })
});
```

Tag for the sync event

Minimum time between successful sync events

Determines battery requirements of the sync; can be either 'auto' or 'avoid-draining'

Determines network requirements for the sync; can be 'online' (default), 'avoid-cellular,' or 'any'

This code is similar to the code in listing 9.1, except you're registering a PeriodicSync. Similar to BackgroundSync, you need to register the sync with a tag name in order to identify how to respond accordingly, and much like BackgroundSync, each tag name needs to be unique to ensure that a different action takes place.

You'll notice that the PeriodicSync API also accepts a value called `minPeriod`. This value is used to determine the minimum time between sync events and is set in milliseconds. If you set the value to 0, it will allow the browser to fire the event as frequently as it wants.

Because syncs will run repeatedly, it's important that the PeriodicSync API take into account the battery and network state of the device it's running on. As developers, we need to be responsible to our users and not drain their battery or generate hefty mobile bills. Configuring properties such as `powerState` can avoid such events because they can either be set to `'auto'` or `'avoid-draining'`. `'auto'` allows syncs to occur during battery drain, but it may be restricted if the device has battery-saving mode enabled. `'avoid-draining'` will delay syncs on battery-powered devices while the battery isn't charging. You can also determine the network usage of a device by configuring the `networkState` property. By setting the value to `'avoid-cellular'`, the browser will delay syncs while the device is connected to a cellular network.

---

[3] https://github.com/WICG/BackgroundSync/blob/master/explainer.md#periodic-synchronization-in-design

'online' will delay syncs if the device is online, and 'any' is similar to 'online', except syncs may happen while the device is offline.

It's worth noting that PeriodicSync isn't meant to be an exact timer. Although the API accepts a minPeriod in milliseconds, it could mean that the sync might not fire exactly on time. All this could be due to network connection, battery state, or the settings of the current device. Due to the nature of PeriodicSync requiring device resources, it's highly likely that it will require opt-in permission from the user.

This is a very exciting feature for the web. I look forward to seeing the exciting things that developers around the world begin to build with it.

9.4 Summary

BackgroundSync is a new web API that lets you defer actions until the user has stable connectivity. It behaves similar to the outbox on an email client—messages are queued up in the outbox and as soon as there's a connection, they're sent.

Tags are useful because they allow you to "tag" a specific event so you know how to respond appropriately in your sync. Each sync needs to have a unique tag name.

You can test BackgroundSync in action by disabling your connection to the network; as soon as you re-connect, your queued syncs will be sent.

Another new API called PeriodicSync allows you to schedule a sync for a predetermined time; it has a number of settings that allow you to schedule how frequently to run, which network connections it can run under, and the allowed battery states of the device to run on.

Part 5

The future of Progressive Web Apps

The web is constantly evolving. It seems like every time I blink, a new feature or library is being released to the web. The growth of Progressive Web Apps (PWAs) is firmly on the radar of browser vendors, and giving web developers access to these new features is part of their roadmap. As a developer, it's an exciting time to be developing for the web. I'm excited to see how the next few years unfold. In this final part of the book, we'll look at a few of the great features that are either in development or are due to arrive in a browser near you very soon.

In chapter 10, we'll dive into a new feature called the Web Streams API, which allows you to stream content to your users. This is important because instead of sending a huge chunk of data all at once to be processed by the browser, web streams allow you to stream the data piece by piece, which means the browser can process it much more efficiently. We'll look into exactly what web streams are and how you can use them to supercharge your page-render times.

Chapter 11 is where I gather together some of the most common questions I get when I speak publicly about PWAs and attempt to answer them as clearly and thoroughly as I can.

The final chapter in this book, chapter 12, is aimed at the future of PWAs. This chapter looks at the amazing Web Bluetooth features that are already available in your browser. We'll also look at other features such as the Payment Request API, Web Share, and one of my favorites, the Shape Detection API.

The future of PWAs is looking good!

Streaming data

10

In part 5 of this book, we'll focus our attention on the future of Progressive Web Apps (PWAs) and the many great features that are coming soon to a browser near you. In this chapter, we'll look at a useful feature called the Web Streams API, which lets you stream content to your users.

We'll dive into what web streams are and how to use them and go through some practical examples that you can apply to your PWAs today. You'll start off by building a basic example using the Fetch API and then graduate to using the Web Streams API within a Service Worker to supercharge the load times of your web pages. If you think your web pages are fast after the earlier chapters, just wait and see how fast they can become.

10.1 *Understanding web streams*

For web developers, there's never been a more exciting time to build for the web. Browsers are more feature-rich and devices more powerful each year. On top of that, we have great frameworks and tooling as well as features such as Service Workers that allow you to build amazing websites for your users. Using the Progressive Times application we've used in the book as an example, you could build a streaming video player or even use the streaming abilities of a browser to progressively render a large web page.

The Web Streams API lets you stream content to your users. For example, say you want to display an image on a web page. Without streaming, the following steps need to take place in the browser:

1   Fetch the image data from the network.
2   Process the data and uncompress it into raw pixel data.
3   Render the results to the page.

All these steps are critical to displaying an image, but why should you wait for the entire image to be downloaded before you can start these steps? What if you could process the data piece by piece as it was downloaded instead of waiting for the entire image to download? Without streaming, you need to wait for the entire contents of the download to complete before you can return a response. But using streaming you can return the results of the download and process it piece by piece, allowing you to render something onto the screen even sooner. The great thing about this is that you can process the result in parallel with fetching—much better.

If you've been following along with the chapters of this book, you may be wondering why you even need the Web Streams API. After all, using Service Worker caching, your web pages are faster and more reliable than ever. That's true, but you aren't taking advantage of the streaming capabilities built into the browser. Imagine for a second that the resource you're retrieving is really large and takes a while to download. Without streaming, you'd have to wait for the entire contents of the resource to be downloaded before you could begin rendering it. With streams you can begin reading from the network, transforming the data, and rendering it onto the screen of your device. Imagine if you could combine caching and streaming together—you'd get an even better result.

Streams also come with many other benefits, one of them being that they reduce the amount of memory that a large resource takes up. For example, if you needed to download a large file, process it, and keep it in memory, that could become a problem. With streaming, you can reduce the amount of memory that a large resource takes up because you're processing the data piece by piece; this feature, known as *flow control*, plays an important role in web streams.

10.1.1 *What's the big deal with web streams?*

It's Friday night and you're watching your favorite TV series on Netflix. Suddenly the internet connection drops, and the film buffers for a few seconds before continuing where it left off. This is a stream in action, and it's using flow control to react to the speed at which data is read from the network. Because the stream reads data piece by piece, it can pick up where it left off.

If that same video is being downloaded and then transformed (decoded) at 200 frames per second, and you only want to display the results of the video at 24 frames per second, you could end up with a backlog of decoded frames, and ultimately your device could run out of memory.

Using flow control, you can use the decoder to detect whether you're producing decoded frames faster than they're being read, which would allow you to slow down the network stream and the rate at which you're downloading. A perfect of example of this is when you watch a Netflix film and it buffers for a few seconds—that's a stream in action.

Web streams also come with a few other benefits:

- *Start/end aware*—Streams are aware of where they start and where they end, although a stream could be infinite, too.
- *Buffering*—Streams can buffer values that haven't been read yet. Without streams, this data would be lost.
- *Chaining via piping*—You can pipe streams together to form an async sequence.
- *Built-in error handling*—Any errors that occur will be propagated down the pipe.
- *Cancellable*—You can cancel a stream, and it can be passed back up the pipe.

10.1.2 *Readable streams*

One of the key concepts of web streams is known as a readable stream. A *readable stream* represents a source of data that you can read data from. Readable streams allow data to come out of the stream and not back in.

Readable streams consume two types of data sources: push sources and pull sources. As the name implies, *push* sources push data to you, regardless of whether or not you're requesting data from them. One of the great things about push sources is that they provide a mechanism for pausing and resuming the flow of data, which is what makes streams so powerful. *Pull* sources require you to request, or pull, data from them. An example of a pull source might be a file handle that allows you to read specific amounts of data or seek a specific location in the file. Readable streams are an easy way to wrap both push and pull sources together in a single, easy-to-understand interface.

You're going to be using readable streams closely (both push and pull) throughout the rest of this chapter, so it's an important concept to understand. You can get started crafting your own readable streams using a few lines of code. The code in the next listing provides a basic example of what a readable stream looks like.

Listing 10.1 A Readable Stream

```
var stream = new ReadableStream({
  start(controller) {},
  pull(controller) {},
  cancel(reason) {}
}, queuingStrategy);
```

Using listing 10.1 as a foundation for your understanding of readable streams, let's look a little closer. The `ReadableStream` class accepts an object passed to the constructor that can implement any of the following methods to determine how the constructed stream instance will behave:

- The `start(controller)` is called immediately and is used to set up any underlying data sources, such as push or pull ones. If you return a promise from this function and it rejects, it will signal an error through the stream. The `pull(controller)` also won't be called until this promise fulfills.

- The `pull(controller)` is called when the stream's buffer isn't full, and it will get called repeatedly until it is full. If you return a promise from this function and it rejects, it will signal an error through the stream. It's also worth mentioning that the `pull(controller)` won't be called again until the promise from the previous `pull(controller)` fulfills.
- The `cancel(reason)` is called when the consumer signals that they are no longer interested in the stream and is used to cancel any underlying data sources.
- A `queuingStrategy` is an object that determines how a stream should signal that it's overloaded based on the state of its internal queue. Earlier in this chapter I mentioned flow control and how it can cause a network stream to notice that it's fetching data faster than it's being read by the decoder and can then slow down the download. Understanding how this works isn't vital, but you should know that you can control it if needed. In this chapter, we'll use the default queuing strategy.

As we progress, you're going to be looking at web streams in action and have a little fun with them.

10.2   *A basic example*

One of my favorite articles about the Web Streams API was written by Jake Archibald from Google. Entitled "2016: The Year of the Web Streams,"[1] it dives into web streams and discusses how they apply to modern web applications. We'll adapt one of the examples in his article slightly and break it down. The example is meant as a fun explainer of web streams and isn't something you'd do in a real-world application. The following listing creates a readable stream and deliberately slows down the data being streamed to the browser, which will result in a page that renders progressively. It's a good introduction to the streaming capabilities of the browser. The code resides in a Service Worker file.

Listing 10.2   **Readable stream that slows down data from the server**

```
self.addEventListener('fetch', event => {
    event.respondWith(htmlStream());
});

function htmlStream() {
  const html = 'html goes here....';

  const stream = new ReadableStream({
    start: controller => {
      const encoder = new TextEncoder();
      let pos = 0;
      let chunkSize = 1;
```

Tap into the fetch event and respond with the HTML stream.

The HTML string you're going to return

You're building a new ReadableStream.

To turn the text into bytes, you need to use a TextEncoder.

---

[1] https://jakearchibald.com/2016/streams-ftw/

Push the
results
onto the
web
stream.

```
function push() {
  if (pos >= html.length) {
    controller.close();
    return;
  }

  controller.enqueue(
    encoder.encode(html.slice(pos, pos + chunkSize))
  );

  pos += chunkSize;
  setTimeout(push, 50);
}

      push();
    }
  });

  return new Response(stream, {
    headers: {
      'Content-Type': 'text/html'
    }
  });
}
```

Check to see if you've exceeded the length of the HTML and close the controller.

Enqueue and encode the next chunk of the HTML.

Force a timeout for 50 milliseconds to slow down the rendering.

Start pushing the results of the stream.

Return the results of the stream as a new Response Object.

Whoa—there's a lot going on in listing 10.2. Let's break it down further. The code will use an HTML string and slowly push each chunk onto a stream that's then passed to the browser. First, you're tapping into the fetch event and responding with the htmlStream() function, which is responsible for creating the streamed response. The htmlStream() function is where the magic happens.

Inside the htmlStream() function, you've created a variable that contains a string with the HTML contents that you're going to return to the browser (I've shortened it for brevity). Next, you're creating a new ReadableStream and calling start() to set up the underlying data source (the HTML string in our case).

Because you want to read the results of the stream as text, you need to use a Text-Encoder() to encode the chunks of HTML that are passed to the browser. The push() function is used to push data onto the stream in chunks, and you're going to use it to slow down the stream. At the top of the push() function, you need to perform a quick check to see whether your current position in the stream has gone past the overall length of the HTML string. If it has, you can close the controller and immediately exit the function.

If you haven't gone past the length of the HTML string, you can then queue the next chunk of HTML that you want to push onto the stream. Next, you move forward one position in the HTML string. You also call a setTimeout() on the push() function, which is used to delay the next occurrence of the push() function by 50 milliseconds. Each time you move forward in the HTML string, the next occurrence will take 50 milliseconds to return, which gives the effect of text slowly being rendered to the screen.

Figure 10.1 shows a visual representation of this code in action.

Figure 10.1   Using web streams, the rendering of the page has been deliberately slowed in order to demonstrate the streaming capabilities of the browser.

You can see from left to right as the page slowly begins to stream the results of the HTML to the browser. This allows the browser to use its streaming capabilities to render the data to the page as it's being received instead of waiting for all the data to be downloaded. In this example, we deliberately slowed down the streaming of data in order to show web streams in action, but in reality you wouldn't normally do this. As we progress through the rest of this chapter, we'll look closely at how you can use the power of web streams to supercharge your page render times.

As always, all the code for this chapter is available on the book's GitHub repository. If you'd like to see this specific example, please head over to bit.ly/chapter-pwa-10.

10.3   *Supercharging your page render times*

Earlier in this book, I mentioned that the Fetch API provides a way to easily make HTTP requests using JavaScript. The API is easy to understand and makes use of promises to keep the code clean and readable. To refresh your memory, the following listing looks at a basic request using the Fetch API.

Listing 10.3   The Fetch API

```
fetch('http://deanhume.com', {          ◁─── The URL to access
    method: 'GET'                                using a GET request.
}).then(function(response) {       ◁───
    // success                              If successful, return
}).catch(function(err) {      ◁───         the response
    // something went wrong
});                            If something went wrong, you
                               can respond appropriately.
```

The code in listing 10.3 makes a GET request for a given URL and then returns the response of the HTTP request. If for any reason something goes wrong, the promise will reject, and you can handle the error accordingly.

Once an HTTP request is successful, the Fetch API lets you read the response of the HTTP request in many different formats, including text, JSON, FormData, blob, or even ArrayBuffer.[2] Using the Fetch API, you can even return the body of the response as a stream, which is perfect for our use case.

The Progressive Times sample application has done a great job of allowing you to use many of the great features of PWAs. It was built using the Application Shell Architecture, which allows you to load the "UI shell" of the app and then dynamically insert the rest of the contents of the page. This approach let you take advantage of Service Worker caching and get something immediately to the page while you waited for the remainder of the contents to download. The only downside of the Application Shell Architecture is that it can't take advantage of the browser's built-in streaming abilities—because chunks of HTML are inserted into a document after the page has loaded. That means you need to use JavaScript to retrieve and insert the main content of the page from the server, which can delay rendering.

Figure 10.2 outlines the basics of the Application Shell Architecture.

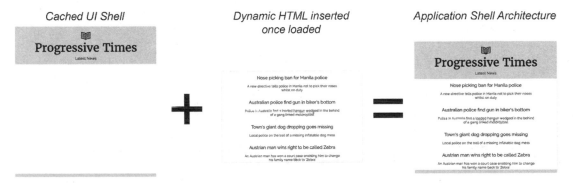

Figure 10.2   The Application Shell Architecture uses Service Worker caching to cache the UI shell and then dynamically fetch and insert the contents into the page after the page has loaded.

The downside is that by using JavaScript to populate the contents of the page, you're bypassing the browser's built-in streaming parser. The more data you're downloading to populate the page, the more it affects the performance of your page rendering because the browser has to wait.

Using web streams, you can approach this slightly differently and stream the contents of the page instead. Doing so would allow the browser to stream the results and start processing and rendering the content immediately, even if it didn't have all of it. Figure 10.3 illustrates this idea.

By using the power of Service Workers combined with streams, you can provide a huge benefit in terms of web performance. In figure 10.3, you can see that using a Service Worker stream you can fetch the different parts of the page and combine them together in one stream. For example, you could add a header, body, and a footer together to make the entire page. This is similar to the method you used with the

---

[2]   https://developer.mozilla.org/en-US/docs/Web/API/Response#Methods

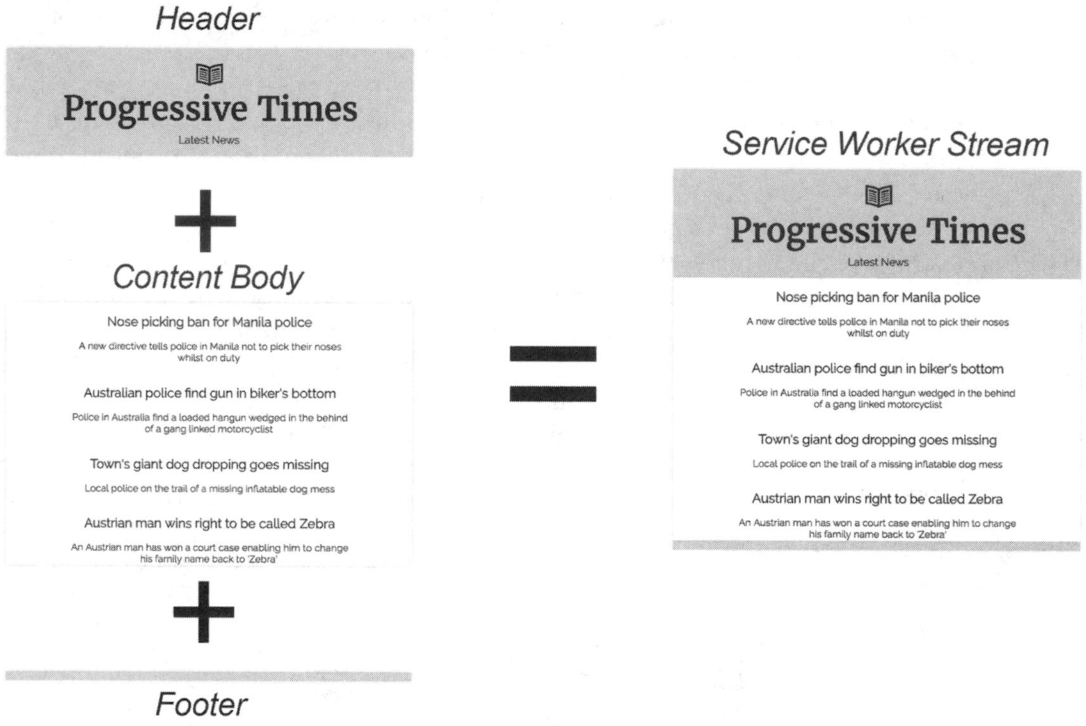

Header

Progressive Times
Latest News

+

Content Body

Nose picking ban for Manila police

A new directive tells police in Manila not to pick their noses
whilst on duty

Australian police find gun in biker's bottom

Police in Australia find a loaded hangun wedged in the behind
of a gang linked motorcyclist

Town's giant dog dropping goes missing

Local police on the trail of a missing inflatable dog mess

Austrian man wins right to be called Zebra

An Austrian man has won a court case enabling him to change
his family name back to 'Zebra'

+

Footer

Service Worker Stream

Progressive Times
Latest News

Nose picking ban for Manila police

A new directive tells police in Manila not to pick their noses
whilst on duty

Australian police find gun in biker's bottom

Police in Australia find a loaded hangun wedged in the behind
of a gang linked motorcyclist

Town's giant dog dropping goes missing

Local police on the trail of a missing inflatable dog mess

Austrian man wins right to be called Zebra

An Austrian man has won a court case enabling him to change
his family name back to 'Zebra'

=

Figure 10.3   Using Service Worker streams lets you fetch the contents you need and then pipe the results to the browser as a stream, which results in instant first render.

Application Shell Architecture, except that you're streaming the whole page content directly from the Service Worker. Content still goes through the regular HTML parser, which means you get streaming and none of the behavioral differences you get with manually inserting content onto the page.

Let's see how to update the Progressive Times web application to use web streams and combine the content using Service Workers. We need to go through quite a lot of code in the Service Worker. The following listing gets us started.

Listing 10.4   Added resources into cache during Service Worker install

```
const cacheName = 'latestNews-v1';

self.addEventListener('install', event => {
  self.skipWaiting();

  event.waitUntil(
    caches.open(cacheName)
    .then(cache => cache.addAll([
      './js/main.js',
      './images/newspaper.svg',
      './css/site.css',
```

Service Worker should start controlling clients that weren't controlled by the previous Service Worker as soon as possible.

Cache the resources during install.

```
        './header.html',
        '/footer.html',
        'offline-page.html'
    ]))
  );
});
self.addEventListener('activate', event => {
 self.clients.claim();
});
```

> Cache the header and footer HTML during Service Worker installation.

> Force the current Service Worker to become the active.

That code may seem familiar; during the Service Worker installation, you're caching a list of important resources that you know will be requested at a later stage. I've also updated the HTML pages of the Progressive Times application in order to simulate server-side rendering—I've removed the Application Shell Architecture and reverted to rendering the page as a whole HTML document.

In listing 10.4, you may notice that both `'header.html'` and `'footer.html'` are being cached during Service Worker installation. This is important because you're going to be combining these pieces of HTML together in your web stream, and it will be much quicker to fetch them from the cache. Next, you're calling `self.skipWaiting()` to force the current Service Worker to become the active one. This in turn fires the activate event and allows the Service Worker to start controlling the page as soon as possible.

Now that the cache is primed, it's time to start consuming this data, as shown in the next listing.

Listing 10.5   Combining HTML in a Web Stream

```
function getQueryString ( field, url = window.location.href ) {
    const reg = new RegExp( '[?&]' + field + '=([^&#]*)', 'i' );
    const result = reg.exec(url);
    return result ? result[1] : null;
};
self.addEventListener('fetch', event => {
   const url = new URL(event.request.url);
  if (url.pathname.endsWith('/article.html')) {
    const articleId = getQueryString('id');
    const articleUrl = `data-${articleId}`;

    event.respondWith(streamArticle(articleUrl));
  }
});
```

> Get the value from the query string.

> Tap into the fetch event.

> Is the incoming route for an article?

> Get the ID of the article.

> Build up a URL of the article.

> Respond with the streaming result.

This code is tapping into the `fetch` event and checking to see whether the current URL is for an article on the Progressive Times application. If so, you need to add a little bit of logic to determine the ID of the article so you can retrieve the correct one from the server.

With this ID, you can then build up an article URL and respond with your stream. One final step needs to take place, and this happens in the following listing.

Listing 10.6   Combining HTML in a web stream response

```
function streamArticle(url) {
  try {
    new ReadableStream({});                          Check to see if the browser
  }                                                  supports the Web Stream API.
  catch (e) {
    return new Response("Streams not supported");     Build a new
  }                                                    ReadableStream.
  const stream = new ReadableStream({
    start(controller) {
      const startFetch = caches.match('header.html');   Retrieve header.html
      const bodyData = fetch(`data/${url}.html`)         from cache.
.catch(() => new Response('Body fetch failed'));         Retrieve the body
      const endFetch = caches.match('footer.html');      of the page using
                                                          the Fetch API.
      function pushStream(stream) {
        const reader = stream.getReader();              Use the pushStream function
        function read() {                               to push the next chunk of
          return reader.read().then(result => {         data onto the stream.
            if (result.done) return;
            controller.enqueue(result.value);
            return read();
          });
        }
        return read();                                  Start fetching the
      }                                                  header data and push
                                                         it onto the stream.
      startFetch
      .then(response => pushStream(response.body))       Fetch the body
      .then(() => bodyData)                              data and push it
      .then(response => pushStream(response.body))       onto the stream.
      .then(() => endFetch)
      .then(response => pushStream(response.body))       Fetch the footer
      .then(() => controller.close());                   data and push it
    }                                                     onto the stream.
  });

  return new Response(stream, {                          Build a new Response
    headers: { 'Content-Type': 'text/html' }            object and return the
  })                                                     results of the stream.
}
```

Retrieve footer.html from cache.

The code in listing 10.6 is the cherry on top of our web stream example. The `stream-Article()` function starts off by testing to see whether the current browser supports the Web Stream API. If it doesn't, you can throw an error and handle accordingly, but if it does you then create a new `ReadableStream`.

In listing 10.4, you primed the Service Worker cache with header.html and footer.html. At this point, you can retrieve them from cache and at the same time use the Fetch API to retrieve the body of the page. Using these three parts, you can stitch them together and pipe the data onto the stream. The great thing about streams is that they're primarily used for piping data from one to another. A readable stream can be piped directly to a writable stream or it can be piped through one or more transform streams first. A set of streams piped together in this way is referred to as a *pipe chain*. In a pipe chain, the original source is the underlying source of the first readable stream in the chain; the ultimate sink is the underlying sink of the final writable stream in the chain. You can see this take place when you call `startFetch()` and then push the results of the body onto the stream. It may seem a bit silly referring to streams as "pipes" and "sinks," but it does stick in the memory how data (like water) can flow from one or more stream to the next.

Finally, you create a new Response object that's used to return the results of the web stream. And that's it—you've created a web stream that renders the contents of your page to the browser and takes advantage of its built-in streaming capabilities. Using Service Worker caching and streams, you've stitched together the page data, meaning you can get an almost-instant first render and then beat a regular server render by piping a smaller amount of content from the network. Content goes through the regular HTML parser, so you get streaming and none of the behavioral differences you get with manually adding content to the DOM. This is a big step forward in terms of web performance and a great way to take advantage of the browser's streaming abilities. To view the code for this example, head over to bit.ly/chapter-10-pwa-streaming.

10.4   *The future of the Web Stream API*

At the time of writing this book, the Web Stream spec is still being developed, which means it's still subject to change. That said, the current functionality already allows you to do some amazing things.

The great thing about being able to tap into the browser's streaming abilities is that you'll start to get access to things in JavaScript such as the following:

- Gzip/deflate
- Audio/video codecs
- Image codecs
- The streaming HTML/XML parser

If you're interested in staying up-to-date with web streams, I recommend keeping an eye on the WHATWG streams document.[3] The future's looking bright for web streams.

---

[3] https://streams.spec.whatwg.org

10.5   *Summary*

Web streams allow you to stream data to your users and the browser to process data piece by piece as it's downloaded.

Without streaming, you need to wait for the entire contents of a download to complete before you return a response. By streaming the data instead, you can return the results of the download and process it piece by piece, allowing you to render something onto the screen even sooner.

Flow control is an important feature of the Web Streams API because it allows you to react to the speed at which data is read from the network.

A readable stream represents a source of data you can read data from and contains two different types of data sources: push and pull.

You can build your own `ReadableStream` by tapping into the `ReadableStream` class and passing it a configurable object.

By combining Service Worker streams and caching, you can supercharge your page render times and use the browser's built-in streaming capabilities.

Progressive Web App Troubleshooting

Whenever I give a talk about Progressive Web Apps (PWAs), there's normally a Q&A session at the end when the audience asks questions or proposes ideas. Often I get asked useful questions that are worth sharing with a wider audience.

In this chapter, I've put together a list of some of the questions I regularly get asked about PWAs and Service Workers and tried to include the most accurate answers I can. Some of these questions may seem obvious, and some not so obvious, but I hope you find them useful.

So here goes, in no particular order: a list of helpful tips, tricks, and gotchas that can help you when you build your next PWA.

11.1 Add to Homescreen

The Add to Homescreen (A2HS) functionality is a great addition to the list of amazing PWA features. Due to some of the built-in tendencies of the browser, this functionality can be tricky to control, but there are a few things you can do that will give you a bit more flexibility.

11.1.1 How do I tell how many users are using the Add to Homescreen (A2HS) functionality on my site?

When the A2HS banner is shown, you can tap into the `beforeinstallprompt` event to determine the choice that the user made when they were presented with the banner. The following listing shows this in action.

Listing 11.1   Determine whether a user accepted or dismissed the A2HS banner

```
window.addEventListener('beforeinstallprompt', function(event) {
  event.userChoice.then(function(result) {

    if(result.outcome == 'dismissed') {

      // They dismissed, send to analytics
    }
    else {
      // User accepted! Send to analytics
    }
  });
});
```

Using listing 11.1, you can determine whether the user dismissed the banner or decided to add your web app to their home screen. Using a web analytics package, you can track their choice and hopefully determine whether this functionality is beneficial to your users.

Another sneaky technique is to set the start URL in your manifest.json file to include a query string indicating that it was opened via the home screen of a user's device. For example, you could update the start_url property on manifest.json, as shown in the following listing.

Listing 11.2   Tracking A2HS usage via a URL in the web app manifest file

```
{
    name: 'Progressive Beer',
    short_name: 'beer'
    start_url: 'index.html?start=a2hs'
}
```

This updated start URL including query string would allow your web analytics tools to track usage and determine how many users are arriving on your PWA via the icon on the home screen of their device.

11.1.2   *The Add to Homescreen banner doesn't make sense for my website—how do I disable or hide it?*

Using the sneaky bit of code in the next listing, you can override the default functionality and cause the browser to ignore the Add to Homescreen (A2HS) banner.

Listing 11.3   Disabling the A2HS banner

```
window.addEventListener('beforeinstallprompt', function(e) {
  e.preventDefault();
  return false;
});
```

Depending on the type of web app, showing this prompt may or may not make sense; perhaps your site covers sensitive topics or a short-lived event, and a prompt may be more annoying than helpful to the user.

11.1.3 *Help, my Add to Homescreen (A2HS) functionality doesn't seem to be working*

Okay, so you've correctly added a manifest.json file to your website and referenced it in the head tag of your HTML like this

```
<link rel="manifest" href="manifest.json">
```

but for some reason you still aren't seeing the Add to Homescreen banner appear at the bottom of the page. There are a few things you may want to check. First, for the A2HS banner to appear, a few criteria need to be met: your site needs to be running over HTTPS, have a valid manifest file (with a start URL and icon) and an active Service Worker file, and the user has to have visited your site at least twice within the last five minutes. The reason for that last one is that if the banner appeared too many times it could be spammy for the user. Those "install our native app" banners are bad enough on some websites already.

11.1.4 *If a user has installed my web app to their home screen, but they clear their cache in Chrome, do my site's cached resources get cleared too?*

Yes, because the PWA experience is powered by Chrome, the storage is currently shared. If a user clears their Chrome cache, your PWA will clear its storage too.

If you'd like to learn more about the improved A2HS functionality in Chrome, I highly recommend learning more about it on the Google Developer's website.[1]

11.1.5 *I'm not sure if my manifest.json file is working correctly—how do I test it?*

One of my favorite tools for validating manifest files is Web Manifest Validator at manifest-validator.appspot.com (figure 11.1). The web app checks the file and uses the W3C specification to determine whether it's valid. If you're having trouble understanding why your web app manifest doesn't seem right, the tool will provide feedback about which character caused an issue along with other things that could be causing the issue.

If you struggle with creating these files and find that you make mistakes here and there, I recommend using a manifest file generator. Bruce Lawson has created a handy tool in which you input your details and it spits out a fully created web manifest file for you. You can find it at brucelawson.github.io/manifest.

---

[1] https://developers.google.com/web/updates/2017/02/improved-add-to-home-screen#will_my_installed_sites_storage_be_cleared_if_the_user_clears_chromes_cache

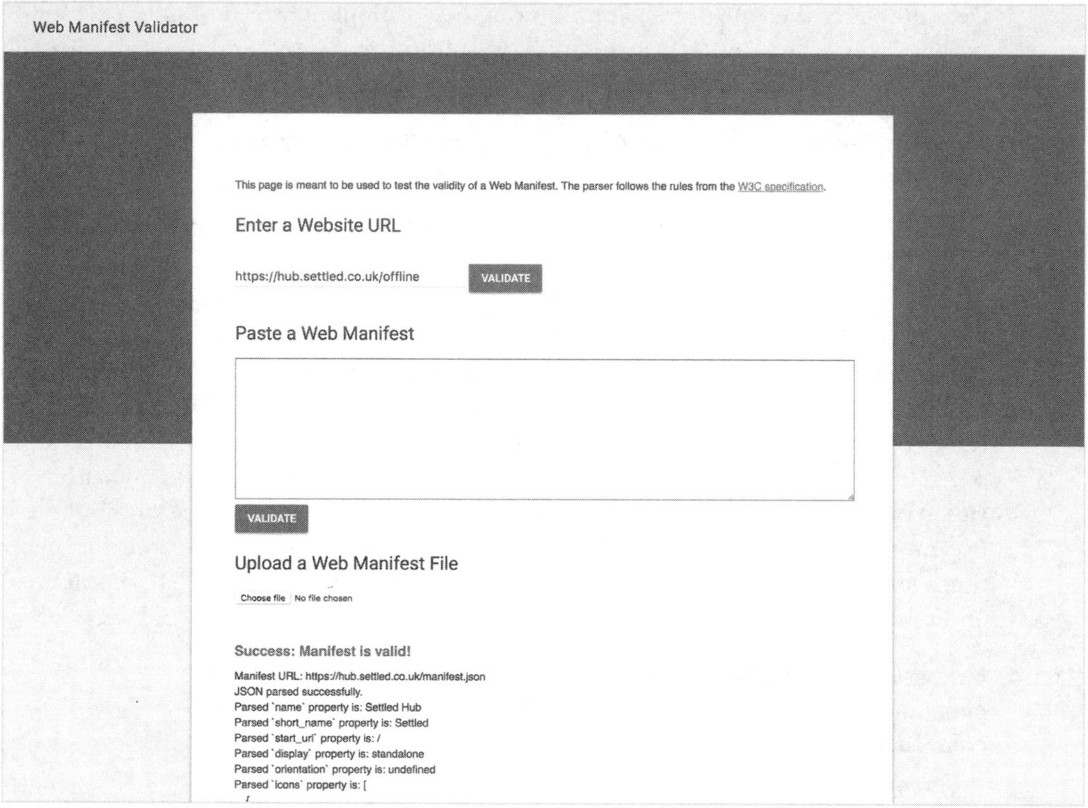

Web Manifest Validator

This page is meant to be used to test the validity of a Web Manifest. The parser follows the rules from the W3C specification.

Enter a Website URL

https://hub.settled.co.uk/offline   VALIDATE

Paste a Web Manifest

VALIDATE

Upload a Web Manifest File

Choose file   No file chosen

Success: Manifest is valid!

Manifest URL: https://hub.settled.co.uk/manifest.json
JSON parsed successfully.
Parsed `name` property is: Settled Hub
Parsed `short_name` property is: Settled
Parsed `start_url` property is: /
Parsed `display` property is: standalone
Parsed `orientation` property is: undefined
Parsed `icons` property is: [

Figure 11.1   If you find that your web app manifest file is incorrect, using Web Manifest Validator can quickly help you diagnose issues.

11.2   Caching

There's a saying that the two hardest things in software development are caching and naming things. This couldn't be truer of Service Worker caching. Getting your resources into cache can be quite straightforward, but with incorrect logic in place, you can quickly cache the wrong resources. This section focuses on troubleshooting Service Worker caching issues.

11.2.1 *I'm adding resources into cache with code in my Service Worker, but the cache isn't updating when I change the file, and why can I still see the older version of my files even after I refresh the page?*

Start by checking the Developer Tools to determine what files are being cached. If you open up Chrome's Developer Tools and click the Application tab, you'll see which files are in the cache, as shown in figure 11.2.

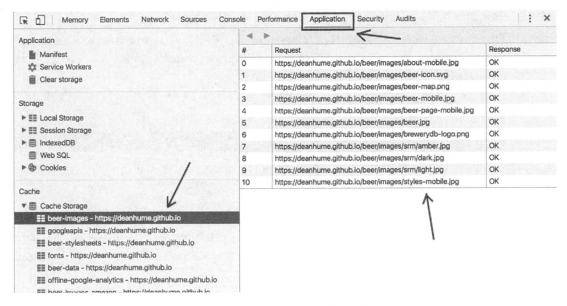

Figure 11.2 The Developer Tools can show what you have stored in cache.

If you need to ensure that files are always updated when you make changes, you may want to consider versioning your files and renaming them. That way you can ensure that each file change is guaranteed to be cached correctly. For example, using file versioning,[2] you may reference a JavaScript file in your HTML like this:

```
<script src="/js/main-v2.js">
```

Each time the file changes, you bump the version, which results in a fresh download.

Another technique to ensure that you always get fresh code is to delete the current cached entries when the Service Worker activates after updating. By tapping into the `activate` event during the Service Worker lifecycle, you can clear the cache. I recommend checking out this code sample[3] for guidance. Depending on how your PWA has been built, you should choose the best strategy to suit your needs.

11.2.2 How do I unit test my Service Worker code?

Testing your Service Worker code can be tricky, but fear not—Matt Gaunt wrote an excellent article on Medium about the ins and outs of testing Service Workers.[4]

---

[2] https://developers.google.com/web/fundamentals/performance/optimizing-content-efficiency/http-caching#invalidating_and_updating_cached_responses

[3] https://googlechrome.github.io/samples/service-worker/custom-offline-page/

[4] https://medium.com/dev-channel/testing-service-workers-318d7b016b19

11.2.3   How much memory can my PWA use on a user's device?

The honest answer is that it really depends on your device and storage conditions. Like all browser storage, the browser is free to throw it away if the device comes under storage pressure.

If you'd like to determine how much storage you have and how much you've used up, the following listing might help.

Listing 11.4   Determining PWA storage usage

```
navigator.storage.estimate("temporary").then(function(info) {
console.log(info.quota); // The total amount in bytes
console.log(info.usage); // How much data you've used so far in bytes
});
```

That code might not work on all browsers, but will definitely point you in the right direction. There's a great answer on Stack Overflow[5] that explains this in more detail.

11.2.4   My cached resources seem to expire every so often—how do I ensure that they stay cached permanently?

When storage space on a device is running low, the browser will automatically clear storage to make more available space. Although this ensures that your user's device runs smoothly, it can make building a truly offline experience for the web a little tougher.

Fear not! There is a way. If you'd like to make cache storage more persistent, you can ask for it explicitly using a bit of code, as shown in the following listing.

Listing 11.5   Persistent cache storage

```
if (navigator.storage && navigator.storage.persist)
  navigator.storage.persist().then(granted => {
    if (granted)
      alert("Storage will persist and not be cleared");
    else
      alert("Storage won't persist and may be cleared");
  });
```

A few criteria need to be met before persistent storage is granted, and to learn more about this great feature, I recommend reading this article.[6]

11.2.5   How do I deal with query string parameters and caching?

When a Service Worker checks for a cached response, it uses a request URL as the key. By default, the request URL must exactly match the URL used to store the cached response, including any query parameters in the search portion of the URL.

---

[5] https://stackoverflow.com/questions/35242869/what-is-the-storage-limit-for-a-service-worker
[6] https://developers.google.com/web/updates/2016/06/persistent-storage

For example, if you make a request for a URL with a query string and it previously matched, you may find that it misses the next time because the query string differs slightly. To ignore query strings when you check the cache, use the `ignoreSearch` attribute and set the value to `true`. The following listing gives you an idea of what this looks like in action.

> **Listing 11.6   Ignoring query string parameters in cache**

```
self.addEventListener('fetch', function(event) {
  event.respondWith(
    caches.match(event.request, {
      ignoreSearch: true
    }).then(function(response) {
      return response || fetch(event.request);
    })
  );
});
```

11.3   Debugging Service Worker–specific issues

Many times I've found myself pulling out my hair trying to figure out the different nuances to Service Workers, only to find that the solution was simpler than it seemed. Hopefully this section will provide the knowledge you need to debug your next Service Worker issue.

11.3.1   How often does the Service Worker file update?

Every time you navigate to a new page that's under a Service Worker's scope, Chrome will make a standard HTTP request for the JavaScript resource that was passed into the `navigator.serviceWorker.register()` call. By default, this HTTP request will obey standard HTTP cache directives, but if the Service Worker file is more than 24 hours old, it will always go to the network and fetch a fresh version of your Service Worker file. This is to ensure that developers don't accidentally roll out a "broken" or buggy Service Worker file that gets stuck in the browser forever—it's like a safety switch for your Service Worker file. For more information, see the article on Stack Overflow[7] where Google's Jeff Posnick goes into more detail.

11.3.2   My Service Worker file is throwing an error, but I'm not sure what's wrong—how do I debug it?

Without a doubt, the easiest way to debug your Service Worker code is to use the Developer Tools in your browser. In Google Chrome's Developer Tools, in the Scripts tab, you can set a breakpoint to help you debug the error, as shown in figure 11.3.

---

[7]   https://stackoverflow.com/questions/38843970/service-worker-javascript-update-frequency-every-24-hours/38854905#38854905

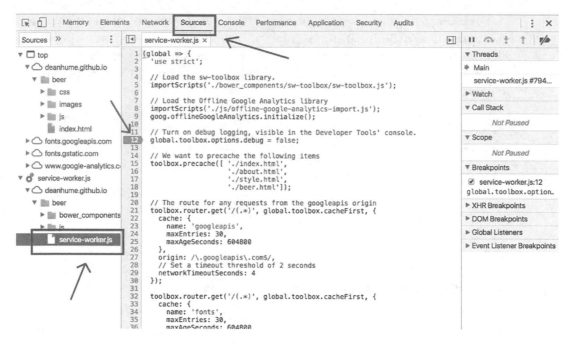

Figure 11.3   Debugging your Service Worker can be a much more efficient way of findings issues in your code logic.

With the breakpoint set in the Developer Tools, your code will pause when it reaches this point and allow you to see exactly how your code logic is executing. Mastering the Developer Tools is a great step forward in becoming a better developer. Although many browser vendors offer tutorials for their developer tools, my personal favorite is one about Chrome's Developer Tools.[8]

11.3.3 Help, I've tried everything, but for some crazy reason my Service Worker logic never seems to execute

It's worth double-checking your Developer Tools to see if you incorrectly enabled a setting. For example, if you enable Bypass for Network, your Service Worker logic will be ignored and instead fetch resources via the network instead of cache, as shown in figure 11.4.

While you're at it, you may want to check that you don't have the other settings enabled when you don't need them. For example, Offline and Update on Reload— I've been left scratching my head many times trying to figure out why my code wasn't working, only to discover that I'd forgotten to disable one of these settings.

---

[8] https://developers.google.com/web/fundamentals/getting-started/codelabs/debugging-service-workers/

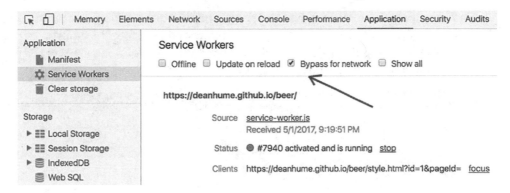

Figure 11.4 If your Service Worker logic isn't executing, consider investigating the settings in your Developer Tools. You may have accidentally overridden something.

11.3.4 I've added code to handle push notifications in my Service Worker file, but how can I test them quickly without writing server-side code?

If you're looking for a quick way to simulate push events within your web app, the Developer Tools provide a quick and easy way to simulate them in action, as shown in figure 11.5.

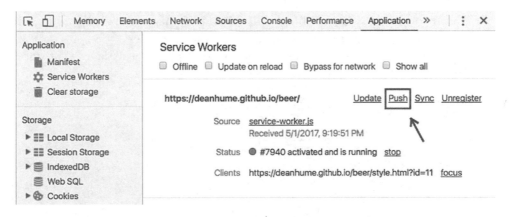

Figure 11.5 Use the Developer Tools in the browser to simulate push events.

11.3.5 I've built an offline web app but now I can't see how users are using it—how do I track usage?

Without a doubt, one of coolest libraries to appear lately has to be the Offline Google Analytics package. Using a bit of clever Service Worker magic, the library will queue up any analytics requests while the user is offline, and as soon as the user regains a connection, it will then send the queued requests through to the analytics server.

To start using the library, you need to include it in your Service Worker file using the code in the following listing.

Listing 11.7   Offline Google Analytics tracking

```
importScripts('../build/offline-google-analytics-import.js');

goog.offlineGoogleAnalytics.initialize();

self.addEventListener('install', () => self.skipWaiting());

self.addEventListener('activate', () => self.clients.claim());
```

By including this code in your Service Worker file, the library will track any actions made by the user while offline, queue them, and then send them in order once the user regains connectivity. Very cool stuff!

11.4 Summary

The Add to Homescreen (A2HS) functionality provides a great addition to your PWA, but it can be tricky to control in certain instances. By tapping into the `beforeinstall-prompt` event, you can control how it behaves.

Using the Developer Tools built into your browser can be a handy way to diagnose and debug any issues you may be having.

If your Service Worker file is older than 24 hours, it will always go to the network and fetch a fresh version of your Service Worker file.

Using the Offline Google Analytics package can be a handy way of tracking your users when they use your PWA offline.

The future is looking good 12

One of the many reasons why I love developing for the web is that the landscape is constantly evolving. Browsers are continually improving, and new features are constantly being released. The future for Progressive Web Apps (PWAs) is looking good: modern APIs allow us to access hardware and sensor APIs, Bluetooth, virtual reality, and so much more. It's an exciting time to be a web developer.

This chapter explores many new APIs that are either in development or are due to arrive in a browser near you soon. We'll look at Web Bluetooth, the Payment Request API, and the Share API. We'll also briefly discuss a few new features that are on the horizon.

12.1 Introduction

As more and more users around the world come online, a large majority of them do so using their mobile devices. In 2015 the International Telecommunication Union estimated about 3.2 billion people, or almost half of the world's population, would be online by the end of the year. Of them, about 2 billion would be from developing countries, including 89 million from the least developed countries.[1]

As a web developer, it's exciting to know that the web is constantly evolving and progressing. Browser vendors are making it easier for us to build fast, resilient, and engaging web applications for our users, regardless of the devices they use. These features enable you to reach many more people and make your web applications accessible for anyone. But remember that not all users out there have the latest,

---

[1] https://en.wikipedia.org/wiki/Global_Internet_usage

fastest devices on the market. This makes PWAs the perfect medium to reach more people; they're lightweight, fast, and work offline.

We'll look closely at new features and APIs that make it easier to build powerful web applications that give us the ability to tap into the hardware on the devices, such as ambient light sensors, proximity sensors, and even accelerometers. But we'll start with Web Bluetooth and sharing directly from the web to the other native applications on your device.

12.2 Web Bluetooth

Imagine the ability to connect to a Bluetooth device from within the browser and interact with the device through a PWA. For example, you could build a web app for your car dashboard or even connect to a set of speakers. Until now, the ability to interact with Bluetooth devices has only been possible for native apps. Fortunately, with the introduction of the Web Bluetooth API, it's now possible using your browser (figure 12.1). The Web Bluetooth API allows web sites to communicate over the Generic Attribute Profile (GATT)—which defines the way that two Bluetooth Low Energy devices transfer data back and forth—with nearby user-selected Bluetooth devices in a secure and privacy-preserving way.

This functionality is relatively new to browsers, but many developers have already started building amazing things using it. For example, developers have built web fitness apps that can interact with heart rate monitors and a web app that can fly a Parrot mini drone.

Being able to interact with Bluetooth devices via the web is easier than you think. The code in the following listing gives you a basic idea of the Web Bluetooth API in action.

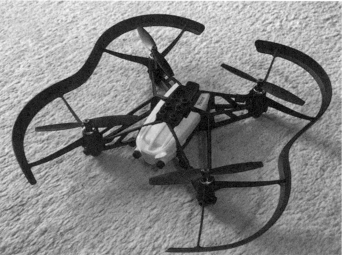

Figure 12.1   Flying a mini drone using the Web Bluetooth API

Listing 12.1 Interacting with Bluetooth devices

```
navigator.bluetooth.requestDevice({          ◁    Request access to nearby
  acceptAllDevices: true,                     ◁    Bluetooth devices.
  optionalServices: ['battery_service']      ◁
})                                                 Accept all devices
.then(device => { console.log (device.name); })    around you.
.catch(error => { console.log(error); });
                                                   Define any optionalServices
                                                   in order to access the
Log the details                                    services of a given device.
of the device.
```

To request access to nearby Bluetooth devices, you need to call the `navigator.blue-tooth.requestDevice()` function and pass it a mandatory object that defines a set of filters. You have to provide these filters in order to request access to specific Bluetooth services that a device might be capable of. The filters can also be used to sort through a list of devices by device name. After all, if you were in a room with 30 Bluetooth devices, it could take a while to search through a list of all of them.

Once the API has been invoked using `requestDevice()`, it prompts the user with a device-chooser pop-up where the user can select the device or cancel. If the outcome is successful, you're returned an object with the characteristics and services of the Bluetooth device, which you can read or write to.

Although this has only scratched the surface of the Web Bluetooth API, you can see how easy it can be to start building your own Bluetooth-enabled web apps. At the time of writing this, the Web Bluetooth API hasn't yet been fully finalized and is currently being implemented in different browsers, but the basic functionality is available for you to start experimenting with today. To learn more about this API, I recommend exploring a few code samples that the Google Chrome team has put together on their GitHub repo at googlechrome.github.io/samples/web-bluetooth.

12.3 *The Web Share API*

If you've ever built a website and needed the ability to share to a social network, you'll know that it's not as easy as it may seem. To add basic share functionality, you often need to include a third-party script and become familiar with its API, and third-party scripts can have a detrimental effect on the page load performance of your site. As you add more sharing links, you'll start to collect a lot of scripts.

As a web developer, I've always been jealous of the ability of native developers to tap into the sharing capabilities of a device. Sharing between native apps on your device is so easy. There's no reason why it shouldn't be as easy for web developers, and this is where the Web Share API comes in. It's a simple API that allows websites to invoke the native sharing capabilities of the host platform directly from the web.

Imagine that a user reads an article on your site and thinks that it's something they want to share with their friends. When they tap the social sharing buttons at the bottom of the screen, instead of another web page, they see a context menu that lets them share using their device's capabilities, as shown in figure 12.2.

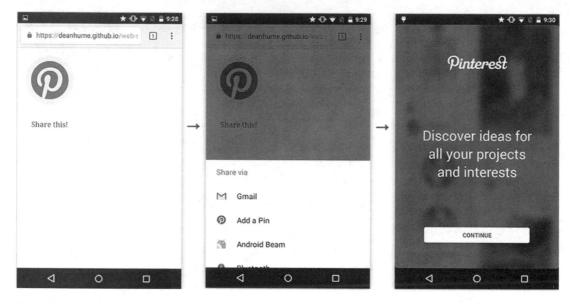

Figure 12.2   The Web Share dialog allows a user to share the current web page with the native apps installed on their device.

In figure 12.2, you can see that when the user taps the Share button, they're presented with a Share Via dialog. Based on their choice, the user can then share with their chosen application.

At the time of writing this article, the Web Share API[2] is currently in trial and only works on Android devices, but it's available for you to start experimenting with. The next listing shows a basic code sample that explains the Web Share API in action.

Listing 12.2   The Web Share API

```
if (navigator.share) {
    navigator.share({
        title: document.title,
        url: shareUrl
    }).then(() => console.log('Successful share'))
    .catch((error) => console.log('Error sharing:', error));
}
```

Check if the Web Share API is supported.

Invoke the web share dialog.

Title of the document to share

URL of the document to share

---

[2] https://developers.google.com/web/updates/2016/10/navigator-share

Let's break down the code in listing 12.2 further. This code resides inside a JavaScript file on your web page. First, it checks to see if the Web Share API is supported in the current browser by checking `navigator.share`. Next, it invokes the share dialog and passes through a document title and share URL. Once the code has been executed, it brings up the native dialog and allows the data to be shared by a native app chosen by the user.

Before you can start testing the functionality, you need to ensure that the site is running over HTTPS, because the API needs this in order for it to function. That's it—if you visit the page on an Android device and tap the Share button, you should see something like figure 12.3.

The Web Share API is a great step forward for web developers because it gives the user control of how and what they want to share with their already-installed native apps. As adoption grows, hopefully this will mean fewer third-party scripts, more native sharing, and ultimately a better experience for the user. Currently this feature is only available on Android, but it would be great to see it adopted by more operating systems. For more on this API, check out its GitHub repository.[3]

Figure 12.3 The Web Share dialog and the available sharing applications

12.4 Payment Request API

When I'm on my mobile device and I'm trying to make a purchase on the go, I'm often wary of the many poor payment implementations out there. I can't tell you how many times I've dropped out of an online purchase on my phone due to tiny buttons, hard-to-read pages, or—even worse—validation errors. Not to mention the security worries I often get when purchasing on a new, unknown website.

This is where the Payment Request API comes to the rescue. It's a system that's meant to eliminate checkout forms by vastly improving the user workflow during the purchase process and providing a more consistent user experience. Its goal is to act as an intermediary between merchants, users, and payment methods. Best of all, the information necessary for a fast checkout can be stored in the browser, so users can confirm and pay—all with a single tap.

If you're on your mobile device and are trying to pay on a website that has implemented the Payment Request API, you might see something similar to figure 12.4.

---

[3] https://github.com/WICG/web-share/blob/master/docs/explainer.md

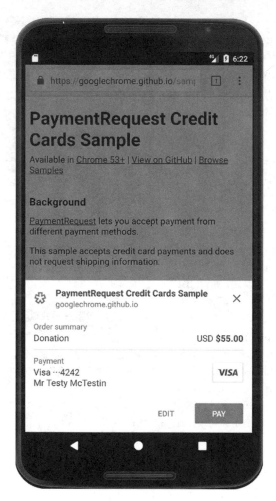

Figure 12.4   The Payment Request API provides an easy-to-use UX that can increase a website's online sales.

The user experience (UX) shown in figure 12.4 provides a much better experience than many e-commerce sites currently offered on mobile devices. This API provides developers with a system that's easy to implement and takes the headache out of building purchase flows that support multiple unique payment methods.

The API is still constantly evolving, but to give you an idea of what a basic example might look like, see the next listing.

Listing 12.3   The Payment Request API

```
if (window.PaymentRequest) {

var paymentMethods = [{
  supportedMethods: [ "basic-card" ],
  data: { supportedNetworks: [ "visa", "mastercard" ] }
}]
```

Check whether the current browser supports the Payment Request API.

Supported payment methods

```
            var details = {
              displayItems: [                    Summary of the order's
                                                 major components
                { label: "Original donation amount", amount: { currency: "USD", value :
                  "65.00" } }
              ],
Total         total:  { label: "Total", amount: { currency: "USD", value : "65.00" } }
amount      }
of the                                                            Invoke the
payment       var request = new PaymentRequest(paymentMethods, details);    Payment
                                                                 Request
                                                                 API.
            request.show().then(paymentResponse => {
              var paymentData = {
                method: paymentResponse.methodName,
                details: paymentResponse.details              Show payment
              };                                              details.
              return fetch('/pay', {
                method: 'POST',
                credentials: 'include',               Data from the
                headers: {                            paymentResponse
                  'Content-Type': 'application/json'
                },
                body: JSON.stringify(paymentData)     The paymentResponse
              }).then(res => {                         resolved correctly.
                if (res.status === 200) {
                  return res.json();
                } else {
                  throw 'Payment Error';
                }                                     Catch any errors
              }).then(res => {                        in the promise
                paymentResponse.complete("success");  chain.
              }, err => {
                paymentResponse.complete("fail");
              });
            }).catch(err => {                                        #J
              console.log("Something went wrong", err);
            });
            }
```

Listing 12.3 looks like a lot of code, but it's much easier to understand when you break it down.

The code starts off by checking to see whether the current browser supports the Payment Request API. Next, you define the supported payment methods such as Visa or MasterCard in a variable named `paymentMethods`. Depending on which credit cards your business supports, this would be the ideal place to include a list of payment methods. Next, you define the information about the transaction in the `details` variable, which includes two major components: a `total`, which reflects the total amount and currency to be charged, and an optional set of `displayItems` that indicate how the final amount was calculated. This parameter isn't intended to be a line-item list but rather a summary of the order's major components: subtotal, discounts, tax, shipping costs, and so on.

Now that you've defined the parameters of the payment, you can invoke the `PaymentRequest()` by passing through the parameters you defined earlier. Next, you activate the `PaymentRequest` interface by calling its `show()` method, which invokes a native UI that allows the user to examine the details of the purchase, add or change information, and pay. A JavaScript promise will resolve and be returned when the user accepts or rejects the payment request.

If the user accepts the payment request, you then pass the details of the transaction through to server-side logic that will handle the payment. Listing 12.3 doesn't include the server-side part of the code because its will vary from business to business and between the different payment methods.

When this code is executed on a browser that supports the Payment Request API, you should see something similar to figure 12.5.

Although the Payment Request API is still very much a work in progress, it provides a standardized UX flow for payments on mobile devices. Things are likely to change

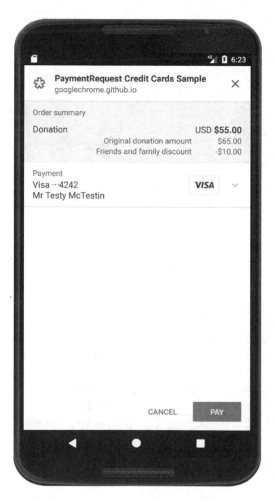

Figure 12.5   The Payment Request API eliminates checkout forms and vastly improves user workflow during the purchase process.

with this API, but it's exciting to see the challenge of online payments being tackled in this way.

For more about the Payment Request API, I recommend checking out the documentation on the Google Developers website.[4] For more working examples and for a chance to try it first-hand, I recommend taking a look at the samples on the GitHub repository.[5]

12.5 Hardware access

Modern browsers are capable of some amazing things: access to hardware features such as the user's geolocation, device vibration, and even battery status are already available via easy-to-access APIs. It doesn't end there, either. More APIs are currently being developed that will give web developers even greater access to device hardware. Modern browser vendors are working on ways to use the hardware features of a device to allow developers even greater access to hardware capabilities. Near Field Communication (NFC), ambient light sensors, proximity sensors, accelerometers, and even shape detection are being targeted by some of the amazing APIs currently being developed.

If you're looking to build a powerful PWA that takes advantage of the hardware on a device, things are only going to get better. Native apps have had access to these features for many years, so it's great to see this kind of thing coming to the web. To give you a taste, we'll look at the Shape Detection API and see a basic example that allows you to detect a barcode from a given image.

12.6 Hardware: the Shape Detection API

The Shape Detection API gives developers access to features such as face detection, barcode detection, and even text detection.[6] This is great for the web.

To understand how you might use it in the real world, consider the following example. Imagine you own a large shop that sells books. If you ever need to check the price of a book without a price tag, you can walk to the register and scan the label to check the price. But if you had a PWA on your mobile device with access to the prices of all the books, you could walk around the store using your mobile device and the barcode detector to quickly and easily give you the price of the book. This is just one example, but being able to detect shapes opens up a world of possibilities.

The following listing shows a basic example.

---

[4] https://developers.google.com/web/fundamentals/discovery-and-monetization/payment-request
[5] https://googlechrome.github.io/samples/paymentrequest/credit-cards
[6] https://wicg.github.io/shape-detection-api

Listing 12.4   Barcode detection using the Shape Detection API

```
var barcodeDetector = new BarcodeDetector();        Invoke barcode detector by
                                                    passing through an image.
barcodeDetector.detect(image)
  .then(barcodes => {
    barcodes.forEach(barcode => console.log(barcodes.rawValue))    Loop through
  })                                                               barcodes and
  .catch(err => {                                                  log their values
    console.log("Looks like something went wrong:", err);         to the console.
  });
```

The code in listing 12.4 gives you a basic idea of the `BarcodeDetector` in action. The code starts off by creating a new instance of `BarcodeDetector`. Nextyou you we invoke the API by calling `detect()` and passing through an image. The image that's passed through needs to be of type `<img>` content, `CanvasImageSource`, `ImageData`, or a blob. If the promise resolves successfully, it will return an array of barcode objects that you can use to extract the raw values from, or even the bounds of the image.

12.7   *What's next?*

This chapter could only touch the surface of some of the great features that are coming to the web. As the adoption of PWAs continues to grow, the web is only going to get better and better.

If you'd like to stay in the loop on the latest features coming to the web, many great resources are available online. I keep a close eye on the web and recommend subscribing to the following websites for regular updates on the world of PWAs:

- Mozilla Developer Network (https://developer.mozilla.org/en-US/Apps/Progressive)
- Google Developers Website for regular updates and new PWA features (https://developers.google.com/web/updates/)
- Opera Developer Blog (https://dev.opera.com/blog)
- https://pwa.rocks on GitHub for a selection of great PWAs
- Awesome Progressive Web Apps on GitHub (https://github.com/TalAter/awesome-progressive-web-apps)

Thank you for joining me on this journey! We've come a long way together. From understanding the basic makeup of a PWA to building one that's super-fast, works offline, and even installs on the user's device—you now know all this is possible from within your browser. I hope you enjoy building your PWAs as much as I enjoyed writing this book.

12.8   *Summary*

The Web Bluetooth API allows websites to communicate over GATT with nearby user-selected Bluetooth devices in a secure and privacy-preserving way.

The Web Share API allows websites to invoke the native sharing capabilities of the host platform directly from the web.

The Payment Request API is a system that aims to eliminate checkout forms by vastly improving the user workflow during the purchase process and providing a more consistent user experience, enabling web merchants to easily implement payment methods.

Modern browsers are capable of some amazing things: access to hardware features such as the user's geolocation, device vibration, and even battery status are already available via easy-to-access APIs.

You can use the Shape Detection API to detect barcodes, text, and even faces inside images.

index

Cross-Platform Desktop Applications
Using Node, Electron, and NW.js
by Paul B. Jensen

> ISBN: 9781617292842
> 312 pages
> $49.99
> May 2017

Angular Development with Typescript,
Second Edition

by Yakov Fain and Anton Moiseev

> ISBN: 9781617295348
> 475 pages
> $49.99
> April 2018

Node.js in Action, Second Edition

by Alex Young, Bradley Meck, and Mike Cantelon

> ISBN: 9781617292576
> 392 pages
> $49.99
> August 2017

For ordering information go to www.manning.com

MORE TITLES FROM MANNING

The Responsive Web

by Matthew Carver

> ISBN: 9781617291241
> 200 pages
> $39.99
> October 2014

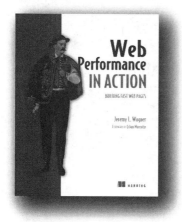

Web Performance in Action
Building Fast Web Pages

by Jeremy L. Wagner

> ISBN: 9781617293771
> 376 pages
> $44.99
> December 2016

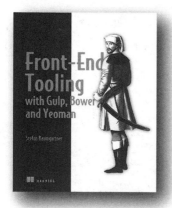

Front-End Tooling with Gulp, Bower, and Yeoman

by Stefan Baumgartner

> ISBN: 9781617292743
> 240 pages
> $44.99
> November 2016

For ordering information go to www.manning.com

Building the Web of Things
With examples in Node.js and Raspberry Pi
by Dominique D. Guinard and Vlad M. Trifa

ISBN: 9781617292682
344 pages
$34.99
June 2016

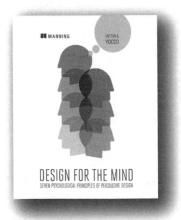

Design for the Mind
Seven Psychological Principles of Persuasive Design
by Victor S. Yocco

ISBN: 9781617292958
240 pages
$39.99
June 2016

Secrets of the JavaScript Ninja,
Second Edition
by John Resig, Bear Bibeault, and Josip Maras

ISBN: 9781617292859
464 pages
$44.99
August 2016

For ordering information go to www.manning.com

MORE TITLES FROM MANNING

Get Programming with JavaScript

by John R. Larsen

> ISBN: 9781617293108
> 432 pages
> $39.99
> August 2016

CSS in Depth

by Keith Grant

> ISBN: 9781617293450
> 450 pages
> $44.99
> December 2017

D3.js in Action, Second Edition
Data visualization with JavaScript

by Elijah Meeks

> ISBN: 9781617294488
> 384 pages
> $44.99
> November 2017

For ordering information go to www.manning.com